C000154347

ZEO

L IVING

R OMANS 12

E VERY

D AY

M ATT SUMMERFIELD

C WR

Published 2020 by CWR, Waverley Abbey House, Waverley Lane, Farnham, Surrey GU9 8EP, UK.
CWR is a Registered Charity – Number 294387 and a Limited Company registered in England –
Registration Number 1990308.

For a list of National Distributors, visit cwr.org.uk/distributors

Unless otherwise indicated, all Scripture references are taken from the *Holy Bible*, New Living
Translation, copyright 1996, 2004, 2015 by Tyndale House Foundation. Used by permission of
Tyndale House Publishers, Inc., Carol Stream, Illinios 60188. All rights reserved.

Other versions are marked:

Jubilee Bible 2000: The Jubilee Bible (from the Scriptures of the Reformation) edited by Russell M.
Stendal. Copyright © 2000, 2001, 2010

NIV: New International Version® Anglicised, NIV® Copyright © 1979, 1984, 2011 by Biblica, Inc.®
Used by permission. All rights reserved worldwide.

The Message: copyright © 1993, 2002, 2018 by Eugene H. Peterson. Used by permission of
NavPress. All rights reserved. Represented by Tyndale House Publishers, Inc.

Concept development, editing, design and production by CWR.

Every effort has been made to ensure that this book contains the correct permissions and
references, but if anything has been inadvertently overlooked the Publisher will be pleased to make
the necessary arrangements at the first opportunity. Please contact the Publisher directly.

Printed in the UK by Linney
ISBN: 978-1-78951-251-9

Contents

What does zeo mean?   5

Embracing the adventure   7

An introduction to Romans   9

01. What has God ever done for us?   13

02. Is Jesus our King as well as our Saviour?   17

03. Which road leads to happiness?   21

04. Transformative thinking   25

05. Understanding God's will for us   29

06. What's so amazing about grace?   33

07. Who do we think we are?   37

08. How much faith do we have?   41

09. What's your unique role?   45

10. Can I help?   49

11. Discovering our God-given gifts   53

12. What's so special about prophecy?   57

13. Are we up for some feet-washing?   61

14. Lessons of faith   65

15. Be a builder-up-er   69

16. We can't out-give a giver   73

17. Leading, or just going for a walk?   77

18. Unselectively kind   81

19. Love without walking on by   85

20. Driven to action by injustice   89

21.	Let's celebrate the good	93
22.	Loving (and liking) other Christians	97
23.	R.E.S.P.E.C.T.	101
24.	No pain, no gain!	105
25.	Have you got zeo?	109
26.	Where's your hope?	113
27.	Playing the waiting game	117
28.	Why is prayer so difficult?	121
29.	Are you ready to help?	125
30.	Entertaining angels	129
31.	Love in the face of intolerance	133
32.	If you're happy then I'm happy	137
33.	Shed a tear before you speak a word	141
34.	Why can't we all just get along?	145
35.	Making friends with 'nobodies'	149
36	No one likes a smarty-pants!	153
37.	No more tit-for-tat	157
38.	Shine bright like a diamond	161
39.	Be a peacemaker	165
40.	Leave it with God	169
41.	Treat your enemies well	173
42.	You can make a difference!	177

What does *zeo* mean?

The apostle Paul writes, 'Never be lacking in zeal, but keep your spiritual fervour, serving the Lord' (Rom. 12:11, NIV). The origin of the phrase 'spiritual fervour' is the Greek word zeo, meaning passion, burning hot, bubbling over, pushing the limits, glowing, holding nothing back, being fully alive or being contagious. Paul is reminding us that as followers of Jesus we need to be living a zeo (passionate) life.

Why? Because to be a follower of Jesus means that we're committed to becoming like Jesus – and Jesus personifies zeo. Jesus is so passionately committed to each and every one of us that He left the comfort and security of heaven, came to our broken world with the power of the kingdom, relentlessly loved, miraculously healed, supernaturally provided, and ultimately gave His life on the cross. Three days later, He rose again so that we can be forgiven, restored into an eternal, life-giving relationship with God and fulfil our original destiny to reflect God in the world. Jesus is passionate about people having God's ultimate life in all its fullness, and we are called to embrace that same passion.

Zeo is the inner fire we carry with us; a passion only God can give within our hearts, that can set the world on fire – if we let it. Through the good times and the bad, in success and struggle, in joys and sorrows, in the loudness and the quietness, this passion burns. And we hold on to God (at times, by our finger tips or the embers of faith) because we know that in Christ alone we find life.

Embracing the adventure

This little book of devotions seeks to explore how each of us can passionately embrace the adventure of following Jesus, because being a Christian is all about Him.

Though Jesus doesn't promise us a life free from pain, He promises to be with us, He promises to get us through the tough times, and He promises that one day He will return and put an end to all suffering and death once and for all. Those who choose Him in this life will get to be with Him for all eternity in the next – in God's perfect, new creation.

Anything is possible with Him!

As we experience true life for ourselves, we discover that this same Jesus has filled us with His Spirit and power and presence for us to share with others. Wherever there is darkness, He can work through us, so that we become His light in the world.

If you haven't already, why not accept His invitation today and pray this prayer at the very beginning of this passionate adventure of following Jesus.

Father God,

I am sorry that I thought I could lead my life better than You. Forgive me for trying to save myself. Forgive me for the things that I say, do and think that bring damage, darkness and death into my life, my relationships and my world.

Thank You that You created me, You know me, You love me and You proved it by Jesus dying on the cross and rising again to rescue me.

Please help me to live the rest of my life with You as my Lord and Saviour. Fill me with Your Holy Spirit every day, and help me to become like Jesus.

Amen.

That's a great prayer to pray every day!

An introduction to Romans

The book of Romans in the Bible is a letter sent to a group of Christians who were living in Rome around AD 57. It was written by a devout Jew called Paul who used to hate Jesus and hate Christians. He did not believe that Jesus was the Son of God. He thought Jesus was a fraud and that Jesus' followers were deluded and dangerous. That was until he had a personal encounter with Jesus Christ, which changed everything. Despite all of his previous scepticism, cynicism and criticism, he came to the realisation – or perhaps we should say revelation – that Jesus was indeed who He said He was.

Jesus Christ *is* the Son of God who broke into human history to show us what God is really like. To show us how to live a perfect human life. To suffer and die on the cross for us. To rise again, and offer each and every one of us forgiveness for our sins, a hope-filled future with God, and, ultimately, freedom from all suffering and sadness. Paul came to this revelation, this life-changing truth, and for the first 11 chapters of Romans he answers the question: 'What should we believe about Jesus?'

Then, in chapters 12 to 16, Paul tackles another important question: 'How do we behave in light of what we believe about Jesus?' Romans 12 is a pivotal chapter in the answer to that question. By plumbing the depths of this fantastic chapter, this series of devotionals aims to inspire and equip us as followers of Jesus Christ.

You can read this book on your own or journey through it with a friend or two. Either way, I hope Romans 12 encourages you in faith as it does me. At the end of each session, you will find:

Read it – an additional Bible passage about the theme.

Think it – a reflective question based on the session's theme.

Write it – space for you to jot down any thoughts from the session.

Pray it – a prayer suggestion.

Live it – a challenge for you to put the session's theme into practice.

Welcome to zeo – living a passionate Romans 12 life!

ROMANS 12:1-21

And so, dear brothers and sisters, I plead with you to give your bodies to God because of all he has done for you. Let them be a living and holy sacrifice—the kind he will find acceptable. This is truly the way to worship him. Don't copy the behavior and customs of this world, but let God transform you into a new person by changing the way you think. Then you will learn to know God's will for you, which is good and pleasing and perfect.

Because of the privilege and authority God has given me, I give each of you this warning: Don't think you are better than you really are. Be honest in your evaluation of yourselves, measuring yourselves by the faith God has given us. Just as our bodies have many parts and each part has a special function, so it is with Christ's body. We are many parts of one body, and we all belong to each other.

In his grace, God has given us different gifts for doing certain things well. So, if God has given you the ability to prophesy, speak out with as much faith as God has given you. If your gift is serving others, serve them well. If you are a teacher, teach well. If your gift is to encourage others, be encouraging. If it is giving, give generously. If God has given you leadership ability, take the responsibility seriously. And if you have a gift for showing kindness to others, do it gladly.

Don't just pretend to love others. Really love them. Hate what is wrong. Hold tightly to what is good. Love each other

11

with genuine affection, and take delight in honoring each other. Never be lazy, but work hard and serve the Lord enthusiastically. Rejoice in our confident hope. Be patient in trouble, and keep on praying. When God's people are in need, be ready to help them. Always be eager to practice hospitality.

Bless those who persecute you. Don't curse them; pray that God will bless them. Be happy with those who are happy, and weep with those who weep. Live in harmony with each other. Don't be too proud to enjoy the company of ordinary people. And don't think you know it all!

Never pay back evil with more evil. Do things in such a way that everyone can see you are honorable. Do all that you can to live in peace with everyone.

Dear friends, never take revenge. Leave that to the righteous anger of God. For the Scriptures say,

'I will take revenge; I will pay them back,' says the LORD.

Instead, 'If your enemies are hungry, feed them. If they are thirsty, give them something to drink. In doing this, you will heap burning coals of shame on their heads.'

Don't let evil conquer you, but conquer evil by doing good.

01

What has God ever done for us?

ROMANS 12:1

*'And so, dear brothers and sisters,
I plead with you to give your bodies to
God because of all he has done for you.'*

The answers are endless. Do you know the very fact that we even woke up today – with breath in our bodies – is a gift from God? Paul reminds us that 'in him we live and move and exist' (Acts 17:28). And that's before we even get started on the fact that Jesus Christ's life, death and resurrection mean that you can be forgiven from your past, experience freedom in your present and be assured of a great future with God for all eternity. Now that's something to be thankful for today.

It's no surprise that Paul kicks off Romans 12 essentially by saying: 'Come on people, God has given everything so that you can have life. I beg, plead, urge and challenge you to fully give your life to Him. It's the only right response!'

In Matthew, Jesus is asked which is the most important of all God's commandments. What's numero uno? Jesus replies, '"love the LORD your God with all your heart, all your soul, and all your mind." This is the first and greatest commandment. A second is equally important: "Love your neighbor as yourself." The entire law and all the demands of the prophets are based on these two commandments.' (Matt. 22:37–40)

Jesus, like Paul, is commanding us to love God with every ounce of our being, to love others compassionately and love ourselves correctly. But what does that look like in practice? Our zeo adventure in the days and weeks that follow will show us what it looks like to say a big YES to God.

READ IT

Read Acts 17:28 again, giving thanks that God is the source of all life.

THINK IT

Is Jesus really number one in your life?

WR**/**TE IT

Make a note of one thing that has struck you from today's reading. List three things that you are grateful to God for.

_____

_____

_____

_____

_____

☐RAY IT

Pray that you will experience greater levels of God's power and presence in your life.

LIV☲ IT

Look for opportunities to pleasantly surprise a stranger with an act of kindness. Remember, God reached out to us, so let's do the same for someone else.

02

Is Jesus our King as well as our Saviour?

ROMANS 12:1
'be a living and holy sacrifice–the kind he will find acceptable. This is truly the way to worship him.'

When you think of Jesus, do you think of Him on a throne or being sacrificed on an altar?

The difference between *altar* and *throne* is that the altar is the place of sacrifice whereas the throne is the place of authority.

It's might be easier to accept the idea of Jesus being our Saviour. We've already mentioned how He died on the cross to rescue us from our sin, and He's always there to bail us out when we need Him. But the idea of Him being our King might be a little trickier. Many of us prefer to be on the throne of our life, treating Jesus as a close adviser.

Yes, Jesus *was* on the altar for us when He died

on the cross, but *now* He is on the throne. 'God elevated him to the place of highest honor and gave him the name above all other names, that at the name of Jesus every knee should bow' (Phil. 2:9–10).

It's time to adjust our thinking. Put Jesus on the throne of our lives and fully surrender ourselves as 'a living... sacrifice' to God. Letting Him be our Lord (which means 'boss') as well as Saviour is truly the way to worship Him. Remember, worship is loving God with our whole being. What's the evidence that we love God like this? Jesus tells us in John 14:23 that we will do what He says. Of course, obeying is not easy, which is why Paul speaks about sacrifice. Someone once said: 'You will only ever know if Jesus is truly Lord of your life if you want to go one way, Jesus wants you to go another way – and you choose *His* way.'

So let's give our lives as a living sacrifice and let Christ be the King of our lives.

READ IT

Read Philippians 2:8–11, making it a prayer for
Christ to be Lord of your life.

THINK IT

*What are the biggest sacrifices you may
have to make as you choose to follow
Jesus every day?*

WRITE IT

Make a note of one thing that has struck you from
today's reading.

_____

_____

_____

_____

PRAY IT

Pray with a trusted Christian friend, who can offer you advice, accountability and support, about areas in your life where you struggle to put God first.

LIVE IT

Make a sacrifice on behalf of a stranger; for example, give up your seat on the train or bus, or instead of buying yourself a coffee, buy a copy of the Big Issue.

WR/TE IT

Make a note of one thing that has struck you from today's reading.

_____

_____

_____

_____

⊏RAY IT

Honestly share with a trusted friend about your struggles with selfishness. Inspire each other to behave differently, and together pray for God's help.

LIV⊏ IT

What could you share with someone this week? Maybe a meal, your time, a book or a cake? Remember, we're blessed in order to be a blessing to others.

04

Transformative thinking

ROMANS 12:2

'but let God transform you into a new person by changing the way you think.'

Buddha is attributed with saying: 'We are what we think. All that we are arises with our thoughts.' That's more true than perhaps we realise! Our thinking shapes who we are and what we do; for example, if we think that the way to be happy is to have loads of money, then we'll spend our lives trying to get rich and famous.

In his brilliant book, *The Life You've Always Wanted**, John Ortberg writes: 'The primary goal of spiritual life is human transformation.' To be a follower of Jesus is to commit to the life-long journey of becoming like Jesus: thinking like Jesus, speaking like Jesus, living like Jesus, loving like Jesus... You get the idea!

Paul encourages us to be 'growing in every way more and more like Christ' (Eph. 4:15). He goes on to remind us that the Spirit 'makes us more and more like him [Jesus] as we are changed into his glorious image' (2 Cor. 3:18).

The Greek word Paul uses for 'changed' is *metamorphoō*, where we get our word 'metamorphosis'. *Metamorphoō* is the same word that Paul uses here in Romans 12:2b when he speaks about our need for God to 'transform' us. This is not a mere personality tweak, but a complete revolution in our nature. Caterpillar to butterfly! How awesome is that? The Holy Spirit is able to work in us to make us brand-new people. A complete change for the better – and it starts in our minds.

So as we read the Word of God, let's allow the Holy Spirit to shape our thinking, and be at work in us every day, making us more like Jesus.

*John Ortberg, *The Life You've Always Wanted* (Grand Rapids, MI, USA: Zondervan, 2004)

REA**⊏** IT

Read 2 Corinthians 3:18. Ask the Spirit to make you more and more like Jesus.

T**⊣**INK IT

How could you develop a habit of regularly reading the Bible and being open to receiving from God's Spirit?

WR/TE IT

Make a note of one thing that has struck you from today's reading.

_____

_____

_____

_____

ᐸRAY IT

Pray that God's Word and Spirit will renew your mind, so that you can be more like Jesus.

LIVᐳ IT

Say something encouraging to someone you meet today.

05

Understanding God's will for us

ROMANS 12:2

'Then you will learn to know God's will for you, which is good and pleasing and perfect.'

What do we think and feel about God's will for our lives? Can we trust that God's will is far better than our own plans? These are the kind of questions that people have wrestled with for years.

Let's start with the second question: Can we trust that God's will is far better than our own plans?

Firstly, Paul tells us that God's will is good. Good as in 'excellent' – in fact, *the best*!

Secondly, God's will is pleasing. By this Paul means 'it makes sense' and is 'acceptable'. (Like a child who opens a Christmas present and cries out: 'Just what I've always wanted!')

Thirdly, God's will is perfect. That's perfect for us – it fits us perfectly because God created us and knows what's best for us.

With all this in mind, accepting and welcoming God's will for our lives seems to make good sense. Why settle for anything less than God's best? But – back to the first question – how do we know what God's will is?

On one level, the Bible has made this very clear. We looked last time at the fact that God wants to transform us to be like Jesus. That's God's primary will for us – that we would be part of His family forever and become like His Son. Becoming like Jesus means that we will grow in our love for God, our love for people and our love for ourselves, in other words, living out the greatest commandment (Mark 12:30–31).

Remember too that this end part of verse 2 rests on all that we've read before. How do we learn to know God's will? By offering ourselves fully to God, making Him boss of our lives (Rom. 12:1); by rejecting selfishness and embracing selflessness; by asking the Holy Spirit every day to help us become more like Jesus – then we 'will learn to know God's will… which is good and pleasing and perfect' (Rom. 12:2).

REA⊂⊃ IT

Read Jeremiah 33:1–3. Why not ask God to 'tell you remarkable secrets'.

T⊢INK IT

How can you grow in trust that God's will for your life is good, pleasing and perfect?

WR/TE IT

Make a note of one thing that has struck you from today's reading.

_____

_____

_____

_____

PRAY IT

Pray that God will continue to reveal His good, perfect and pleasing will to you every day.

LIVE IT

Do a secret act of random kindness for your next door neighbour today – remembering that Jesus tells us to love our neighbour as ourselves.

06

What's so amazing about grace?

ROMANS 12:3

'For by the grace given me' (NIV)

John's Gospel tell us that Jesus is 'full of grace' (John 1:14) while Psalm 103:8 reminds us that 'the LORD is compassionate and gracious, slow to anger, abounding in love.' This word 'grace' is rich in meaning and Paul (the writer of Romans 12) could simply never get over the wonders of God's grace. So what does it mean?

Grace means God's loving kindness – a sacrificial, servant-hearted love that motivates us to do something good for someone else. That's what Jesus is like. He prays for people. He heals people. He feeds people. He gives thirsty people a drink. He listens to people. He weeps with people. He makes time for people. He saves people. Grace is God's loving kindness. But that's not all!

Grace also means God's undeserved favour –

where God does wonderful things for us despite the fact that we don't deserve it. That's radical and that's what Jesus is like. God expresses His loving kindness to us even though we've done nothing to deserve it. In fact, we don't deserve it at all.

Finally, grace means God's excessive generosity – going the extra mile and then some more; for example, sending His Son to die for us on the cross. The cross is the ultimate evidence of God's grace – His loving kindness, undeserved favour, excessive generosity – towards us. May God help us to become a channel of His grace to others.

REA⊂ IT

Read Psalm 103:8. Let God's grace soak in as you meditate on these words.

T⊢INK IT

What makes it difficult for you to accept and receive God's grace?

WR/TE IT

Make a note of one thing that has struck you from today's reading.

_____

_____

_____

_____

⊏RAY IT

Pray that you will receive a fresh experience of God's grace.

LIV⊑ IT

Be excessively generous today with someone who perhaps doesn't deserve your kindness. Experience for yourself the blessing of living a life of grace.

07

Who do we think we are?

ROMANS 12:3
'I give each of you this warning: Don't think you are better than you really are. Be honest in your evaluation of yourselves'

If you were to describe yourself to someone, what words would you use? If friends were to describe you to others, what would they say about you?

Regardless of others' opinions, how do we make sure we have a right view of ourselves, particularly bearing in mind that Jesus calls us to 'Love your neighbor as yourself' (Mark 12:31)? Jesus knows that we will struggle to love others if we don't have a right view of ourselves.

Some of us think we're worse than we actually are – but actually we're probably not as bad as we think.

Some of us think we're better than we actually are – but actually we're probably not as good as we think we are.

By saying, 'Don't think that you're better than you really are', Paul is challenging us to have a right estimation of ourselves, according to what God says. It's God's opinion that counts.

We might feel broken but we are precious to God (Dan. 9:20–23). We make mistakes but we are forgiven by God (Psa. 103). We suffer but we are never forgotten by God (Isa. 49:15). We might be a long way from being perfect – but that's because we're still works-in-progress (Phil. 3:12–14).

Let's not be smug or satisfied about who we are, nor depressed or downhearted about who we're not – because we are God's workmanship, created in Christ Jesus, to do awesome works that God planned for us long ago (Eph. 2:10). Now that's something to be excited about and thankful for!

REA⊏ IT

Read Philippians 2:3–11. How does Jesus' humility challenge you?

THINK IT

What stops you from believing that you are a beloved child of God?

WRITE IT

Make a note of one thing that has struck you from today's reading.

_____

_____

_____

_____

PRAY IT

Pray that in your work-in-progress journey, you will become more like Jesus.

LIVE IT

Have you fostered a negative opinion about someone?
Go out of your way to serve them today.

08

How much faith do we have?

ROMANS 12:3

'measuring yourselves by the faith God has given us.'

The Bible tells us that 'faith is confidence in what we hope for and assurance about what we do not see' (Heb. 11:1, NIV) and, according to today's verse, God gives His children a level of faith.

This is not a *blind* faith but a *reasonable* faith. A conviction that the overwhelming evidence around us points to the reality of a loving, creator God who knows us and wants us to know Him.

But what if we feel that our faith is fragile or almost non-existent? Well, Jesus reminds us that even a *tiny* amount of faith can achieve impossible things for God. Mustard-seed faith can move mountains (Matt. 17:20). But our faith doesn't have to stay small; it can grow. Elsewhere in Matthew, Jesus also tells us that the kingdom of God 'is like a mustard seed planted in a field. It is the smallest of all seeds, but it becomes the largest of garden plants; it grows into a tree, and birds come and make nests in its branches' (Matt. 13:31–32).

Our faith isn't supposed to remain tiny for the rest of our lives; it's supposed to grow rapidly into something much larger, something that affects the whole environment! And the Bible reminds us that it is impossible to please God without faith (Heb. 11:6).

So how do we grow our faith?

- Reading the Bible – which will help us grow in our understanding of God.
- Praying – which will help us grow closer to God.
- Asking the Holy Spirit to help us become more like Jesus.
- Sharing our faith with others through words and actions.
- Hanging out with other Christians who will cheer us on in our faith – in the good and bad times.
- Doing what God tells us to do, even when we want to do something different.

So let's thank God for the faith we have now, and ask Him to help us grow our faith from a tiny seed to a large tree.

REAᗡ IT

Read Hebrews 11:6. Ask God to build your faith, so you can please Him more.

THINK IT

Looking back on your life, how has your faith grown for you personally – each month, each year, each decade?

WR/TE IT

Make a note of one thing that has struck you from today's reading.

_____

_____

_____

_____

⊏RAY IT

Pray that your faith will grow steady and strong in Christ.

LIVE IT

What could you do today that will stretch your faith in Christ? Perhaps an act of kindness or a bold word of knowledge?

09

What's your unique role?

ROMANS 12:4-5
*'Just as our bodies have many parts
and each part has a special function,
so it is with Christ's body.'*

The book of Romans was written during a time
when there was a very clear divide in the religious
community, between the priests and the laity
(ordinary people). The priests were considered to
be the important people who did most of the work
and the laity just needed to show up and listen.
Paul challenges that thinking by stating that a
healthy body is made up of many parts and *every*
part is important, each one has a special function
in the body.

 The Greek work for 'function' is *praxis*, which is
more commonly translated as 'works' or 'deeds'.
Paul is saying that there is a unique role – a unique
work – that everybody in the community of faith

must play. *Everyone* is needed. *Everyone* has their place. *Everyone* is important.

We all have a unique mix of strengths, talents and personality types. God has made us a diverse people for a reason, only *you* can do what *you* can do, which is why Paul stresses in 1 Corinthians 12:12–31 about the need for the body to have eyes, ears, feet and so on. A healthy body is a diverse body – where everyone is bringing their unique contribution.

Sometimes we might want to be 'ears', when God has made us 'eyes'. For example, we might want to be a missionary abroad one day but have the opportunity and skills to work with local young people now. It's helpful and more productive to focus our time, energy and passion on what we *can* bring, rather than being jealous or disappointed about what we can't. There's a place for everyone in the body of Christ and if we don't step up into our unique place then the body will not be whole or healthy.

So let's not be on the outside of the family of God, looking in – let's identify our gifts and passions and offer them to the Church and our community this week.

REAↃ IT

Read 1 Corinthians 12:6. Thank God that we all have a unique part to play.

T⊢INK IT

How can you develop the gifts and talents that God has given you?

WR/TE IT

Make a note of one thing that has struck you from today's reading.

_____

_____

_____

_____

PRAY IT

Pray that God will use your gifts and talents for kingdom impact.

LIVE IT

Do something you love to do for the benefit of someone else; for example, if you love baking, why not bake a cake for a friend? Let your gifts and passions be a blessing to someone in a practical way.

10

Can I help?

ROMANS 12:5
'We are many parts of one body, and we all belong to each other.'

When the poet John Donne wrote 'No man is an island', he meant that we're not supposed to do life by ourselves. We all need people around us to help and cheer us on – and we're to do the same for others. We belong to each other.

We've already considered the importance of recognising that each of us has a unique role to play in the body of Christ, the Church. However, it's good to do this without separating ourselves from others, becoming so individualistic and focused on doing 'my thing' that we don't support others as they seek to do 'their thing'.

In 1 Corinthians 12:21, Paul makes the point that *no* part of the body can say to another, 'I don't need you' or 'I'm not interested in you'. The body works most effectively when every part is working together. We are all different but we are all united. Every member of the body is dependent on every other member. We work together in unity so that the body, the Church, is healthy.

Sometimes I've heard Christians say: 'I don't need to be a part of a church, I've got my relationship with God.' But maybe God would disagree with this kind of thinking. Right there in the beginning of Genesis, God spotted the first thing that was 'not good' (Gen. 2:18). And what was it? That man was alone. Alone? How could Adam be alone? He had God – and surely God was everything Adam needed? Yet the reality is that God knew that Adam needed help from those just like him. We need God *and* we need other people too. It's the way we're wired. So God created Eve to help Adam fulfil his potential in the world, and Adam's job was to do the same for Eve.

The Church is not a building or a service or a ministry. The Church is the family of God, serving God. And to that end we belong to each other and serve together. How do we do this in practice?

- By not having a consumer attitude towards churches, but asking what we can do for our church.
- By thinking the best of people and giving them the benefit of the doubt. Choosing to take the low ground, rather than getting on a high horse!
- By opposing gossip and rumours, and pursuing unity, forgiveness and reconciliation.

REA⊐ IT

Read Psalm 133:1. Reflect on how you can foster an atmosphere of unity in your church through your words and actions.

T⊢INK IT

Many families have their difficulties – including the Church family. So how can you keep growing in love for the Church that Jesus gave His life for?

WR/TE IT

Make a note of one thing that has struck you from today's reading.

_____

_____

_____

_____

PRAY IT

Ask God to reveal to you ways in which you can show your appreciation for others.

LIVE IT

Go out of your way to encourage someone who heads up a work in your church – even better, maybe offer to help for one week!

11

Discovering our God-given gifts

ROMANS 12:6

'In his grace, God has given us different gifts for doing certain things well.'

It was Eric Liddell, the famous 1920s Olympic athlete, who once said: 'I believe God made me for a purpose, but He also made me fast. And when I run I feel His pleasure.'

I passionately believe, like Paul in Romans 12:6 – and Eric Liddell – that everyone is created by God with certain skills and talents, which can be nurtured and developed. It just seems that some people are naturally athletic, or natural singers, or natural dancers or naturally intellectual. There is something in the way that God has wired them to be talented and skilled in these areas.

God has given each of us natural talents and skills that we can use for His service, to serve other people. How do we discover our natural talents? They tend to be the things we really enjoy doing. The things that help us feel alive and fulfilled, whether it's writing, cooking, caring, singing, organising... the list goes on.

In Ephesians 4:7, Paul makes a similar point when he writes that God 'has given each one of us a special gift through the generosity of Christ.' But over and above the natural talents God has given us, Paul is more specifically talking about God giving us spiritual gifts. (It's the Greek word *charisma* that is translated as 'gifts' in Romans 12:6 and Ephesians 4:7.)

Spiritual gifts are extraordinary abilities that God gives us, through the Holy Spirit, to serve people. Sometimes we call them *grace* gifts, which means we don't deserve them, but because God loves us and because He is so generous and kind, He gifts us with supernatural abilities in order to make a difference in the world. Read 1 Corinthians 12 and Ephesians 4 for a closer look at the spiritual gifts. So what needs to be our attitude towards spiritual gifts?

- To be hungry for the gifts (1 Cor. 14:1).
- To use the gifts to serve people (1 Pet. 4:10).
- To develop and nurture the gifts (2 Tim. 1:6).

Let's recognise and use the natural gifts that God has given us and pray that they will positively impact the world.

REA⊂⊃ IT
Read 1 Corinthians 14:1. Pray that your passion for spiritual gifts increases.

T⊢INK IT
What gifts do you believe God has, in His kindness, given you and how can you keep growing in them?

WR/TE IT
Make a note of one thing that has struck you from today's reading.

_____

_____

_____

_____

55

PRAY IT

Pray that God will release more of His spiritual gifts into your life.

LIVE IT

Ask God for a spiritual gift (eg wisdom, knowledge, prophecy, serving, healing, miracles or hospitality) and try to exercise it for the benefit of somebody else today.

12

What's so special about prophecy?

ROMANS 12:6

'So if God has given you the ability to prophesy, speak out with as much faith as God has given you.'

Many people have questions regarding the gift of prophecy. What is it? Should it still be happening? Could God use *me* to prophesy? How do I know if a prophecy is from God? What if I get it wrong and damage people? These are all valid and important questions to grapple with.

Paul encourages us to 'eagerly desire the gifts of the Spirit, especially prophecy' (1 Cor. 14:1, NIV). For some reason, Paul singles out prophecy and encourages followers of Jesus to be hungry for this gift above all others. It's also the first gift he mentions in Romans 12.

So what's so special about prophecy? It's the God-given ability to speak out a word from Him that brings strength, encouragement and comfort. It can be for the past, the present or the future. It's no surprise, then, that Paul encourages believers with this gift to 'speak out'. We all need to hear from God, don't we? The gift of prophecy is primarily for the benefit of others. Sometimes God wants to speak to us, other times He wants to speak through us.

I was once praying with a guy and I felt God was saying that his ministry was like a 'best kept secret' but the secret was about to burst out. When I finished praying, he told me this was absolutely the 'word' he needed. He was blown away and I was really encouraged that God had graciously used me to speak a prophetic word to him – and it all happened very naturally in prayer. As a result, my faith grew and I was encouraged to be open to words of prophecy again.

This is what Paul means when he talks about prophesying in accordance with our faith. Let's ask God to use us prophetically, and take some small steps of faith. As we grow in encouragement, we'll grow in faith and God will use us more. How awesome is that?

Four things to remember with prophecy:

1. God will never say anything that contradicts the Bible or His character.
2. Invite other people you trust to 'weigh up' your word from God.
3. If you love people, you'll never go far wrong, even if you haven't quite heard from God right.
4. Don't take the Lord's name in vain. It's much better to say: 'I believe that God might be saying...' than: 'God is saying...'

REA⊂ IT

Read 2 Peter 1:20–21.

T⊣INK IT

What struggles do you have when it comes to discerning God's voice, and how can you overcome them?

WR/TE IT

Make a note of one thing that has struck you from today's reading.

_____

_____

_____

_____

PRAY IT

Pray that, like the prophets, you will be 'moved by the Holy Spirit' (2 Pet. 1:21).

LIVE IT

Take a step of faith and ask God for a prophetic word for someone you know. At an appropriate moment, sensitively share it with them.

13

Are we up for some feet-washing?

ROMANS 12:7
'If your gift is serving others, serve them well.'

John 13 tells us the famous story of Jesus washing the feet of His disciples. This was a job normally reserved for the lowliest of servants. After all, unless you're a chiropodist, most people don't go around touching people's feet – particularly if they're covered in mud, sand and camel poo. But in this powerful moment, on the eve of His death, Jesus reminds us that He is a *servant* king. He is our example and reminder that to lead is to serve.

What does God require of us? 'He requires only that [we]... serve him with all [our] heart and soul' (Deut. 10:12). And how do we serve God? By serving others.

John reminds us that serving means being needs-aware and action-oriented: 'If anyone has material

possessions and sees his brother in need but has
no pity on him, how can the love of God be in that
person?' (1 John 3:17, NIV). We can't say we love
God if we ignore the needs of those around us. We
need to be people who have an inbuilt radar for the
needs of others and then the commitment to do
something about it.

Regretfully, there have been many times when I
have walked past a person selling the *Big Issue* and
never bought a copy. I could easily spare a few quid,
and a prayer, for this person who is far worse off
than me but too often I just walk by.

Jesus also tells us, in Matthew 6:1-4, that we
must ensure we serve with the right motives.
Our intention shouldn't be to bring attention
to ourselves, to make ourselves look good or
to feed some inner ego trip. We need to view
serving as being part of our worship to God,
responding to the need, often in secret and never
expecting praise or recognition. Paul says, 'Serve
wholeheartedly, as if you were serving the Lord,
not people' (Eph. 6:7, NIV). Give it everything we've
got. It's what Paul is also talking about when he
says 'serve them well' (Rom. 12:7). This means it
should cost us something. Serving always involves

sacrifice. Just as it did for Jesus when He died on the cross.

Finally, Peter tells us in 1 Peter 4:11 that we serve in God's strength. This isn't just an act of will. It's a daily invitation where we ask God for His compassion, commitment and courage to help us step outside of our comfort zone and serve others. When this is our prayer, we can be assured that the Holy Spirit will come alongside us, helping us and making us more like Jesus who came to serve.

Let's commit to being a servant of God, for the benefit of others, and ourselves.

READ IT
Read Mark 9:35.

THINK IT
How do you think God might work through your talents and passions to serve others?

WR/TE IT

Make a note of one thing that has struck you from today's reading.

_____

_____

_____

_____

PRAY IT

Pray that God will help you be the servant of all people.

LIVE IT

Go out of your way today to serve someone you don't know; for example, buy a Big Issue, put a gift on someone's doorstep or leave some flowers on someone's car.

14

Lessons of faith

ROMANS 12:7

'If you are a teacher, teach well.'

Did you have a favourite school teacher? As I look back on my favourite school teachers, I think the following attributes made them stand out from the rest:

- They knew their subject, loved their subject and communicated it creatively.
- They were firm but always fair: prepared to discipline, but only to bring out the best in us.
- They genuinely cared about us. Teaching was not a job for them: it was a calling.

In Matthew 7:28, we're told that the crowds were amazed at the teaching of Jesus. They recognised that He was an exceptional communicator and that He taught as one who had an authority that other teachers of the day simply didn't have. So what was that authority, and what can we learn from His way of teaching as we seek to help others?

It was clear that Jesus knew and loved teaching about the kingdom of God. He spoke about it all the time and – better still – He embodied it. Jesus didn't just speak out the message, His whole life *was* the message.

He was also incredibly creative in His communication, making use of a range of teaching tools, including powerful stories, symbolic lessons and provocative one-liners. He always tailored His communication to His audience. He started where they were.

Jesus was 'full of grace and truth' (John 1:14, NIV). He deeply loved people, which was why He confronted them with the reality of their broken choices. Jesus was never interested in simply imparting information, but taught for transformation.

While some of us might have a genuine sense of calling and gifting as teachers, all of us are learning lessons about faith and life that we can share with others. We can be great teachers of others when we:

- Love God and believe wholeheartedly in our message.

- Know and communicate our message well by taking time to study and pray about it.
- Live out our message through our actions and by loving people.
- Allow the power of the Holy Spirit to ultimately bring powerful transformation.

Even Paul, who wrote much of the New Testament, admitted that he needed the help of the Holy Spirit when preaching: 'I came to you in weakness— timid and trembling. And my message and my preaching were very plain. Rather than using clever and persuasive speeches, I relied only on the power of the Holy Spirit. I did this so you would trust not in human wisdom but in the power of God' (1 Cor. 2:3–5). This is an important reminder that the real power in our sharing comes from the Spirit. We trust God to bring the transformation in people's lives.

REA⊐ IT
Read 2 Timothy 2:2.

TH—INK IT

What are some of the important faith and life lessons that you've learnt?

WR/TE IT

Make a note of one thing that has struck you from today's reading.

_____

_____

_____

_____

□RAY IT

Pray that God will help you to teach others to follow Jesus.

LIV≡ IT

Think of a creative way that you can teach someone about the love of God.

15

Be a builder-up-er

ROMANS 12:8

*'If your gift is to encourage others,
be encouraging.'*

The Duke of Wellington was renowned for being
the hard-nosed military leader who defeated
Napoleon at Waterloo. He was once asked, in his
old age, what he might do differently if he could live
his life all over again. 'I'd give more praise,' was his
thoughtful response. 'I'd give more praise.'

It was the American philosopher and psychologist
William James who said: 'The deepest principle in
human nature is the craving to be appreciated.'

What's the message here from the Duke,
from William James and from Paul? Simply this:
everybody needs encouragement, praise and
appreciation. Everybody should commit to grow in
the gift of encouragement, because 'to encourage'
literally means 'to put courage into' someone – and

we all need courage from time to time, don't we?

Think for a moment about what it means 'to appreciate'. When we say that the value of a house has 'appreciated', we mean that the house has gone up in value. That's what happens when we appreciate people: they feel increasing value and worth.

The Greek word for 'encourage' that Paul uses in today's verse is *parakaleō* and it means 'to come alongside someone and strengthen them'. It's reminding someone that they're not alone. That you are with them. That you believe in them. That you want to see them become all that God created them to be. That's why Paul reminds us that our job in life is to 'build each other up' (1 Thess. 5:11). And again in Ephesians: 'Do not let any unwholesome talk come out of your mouths, but only what is helpful for building others up according to their needs, that it may benefit those who listen.' (Eph. 4:29, NIV). If someone lacks regular encouragement, the writer to the Hebrews tells us that their heart becomes hard (Heb. 3:13). So we all need to improve in this, don't we? Too often our words and actions damage, rather than develop, people. But that can all change, starting from now. Let's be an encourager!

REAⅭ IT
Read Psalm 138:3.

TⅢINK IT
Which aspect of your life do you need encouragement in today?

WR**/**TE IT
Make a note of one thing that has struck you from today's reading.

⯀RAY IT
Pray that God will be your encouragement today.

LIVE IT

Encourage a friend by telling them what it is you appreciate about them. Maybe you will be able to notice an increase in their self-worth as a result.

16

We can't out-give a giver

ROMANS 12:8

'If it is giving, give generously.'

When Howard Hughes (the billionaire pilot, film producer and businessman) was once asked how much money was needed to make someone happy, he apparently quickly replied: 'Just a little bit more!' And yet, later in life, he began to recognise the truth that money can't buy happiness.

Of course we all need money in order to live but the pursuit of money will never satisfy us, which is why the Bible places such a great emphasis on *giving* rather than *getting*. Jesus, quoted by Paul, said, 'It is more blessed to give than to receive.' (Acts 20:35, NIV).

There's just something about the power of giving that releases us from the grip of selfishness, freeing us to be content with what we have while also experiencing the joy of helping others. Like today's verse, Proverbs 11:25 also reminds us to give generously. We're blessed by God to be a blessing to others.

We also need to give sacrificially; giving has to cost us something. The churches in Macedonia went without stuff so that the work of God could grow (2 Cor. 8:1–5). I have some good friends who used to have two cars but have downsized to one car. It's a sacrifice and a struggle but they're doing it to save money for a once-in-a-lifetime holiday. Maybe you've done something similar. I know I have. But when was the last time I went without something in order to bless someone else or so that the kingdom of God could grow?

Paul tells us to give cheerfully (2 Cor. 9:7). Let's be thrilled that we are in a position to help others. Let's not give begrudgingly or with wrong motives, but with a genuine smile on our face because we're grateful to God that we are able to meet a need.

Jesus also challenges us to give secretly (Matt. 6:1–4). Blessing someone is not an opportunity to blab to the world about how generous we are. When we give secretly, the only recognition we'll get is from God, which is the best recognition to get. Otherwise we're in danger of looking for the 'thank you' from someone; looking for them to love us more because we're so generous; or looking for them to reciprocate. Far better to give in secret.

So let's give, remembering that we can't out-give a giver. God has blessed us beyond our wildest dreams with His love, forgiveness, presence, kindness, hope, provision... the list goes on! His generosity towards us is unparalleled – and it never stops.

REAⅮ IT
Read 2 Corinthians 9:8. Thank God for His provision in your life.

T⊣INK IT
How can you keep going and growing in a generous lifestyle?

WR/TE IT

Make a note of one thing that has struck you from today's reading.

_____

_____

_____

_____

⊏RAY IT

Pray that God will give you a desire to be generous.

LIV⊟ IT

Do something ridiculously generous this week that really costs you something and keep it a secret between you and God alone.

17

Leading, or just going for a walk?

ROMANS 12:8
*'If God has given you leadership ability,
take the responsibility seriously.'*

Someone once said: 'If you're leading but no one is following, then you're just going for a walk.' Harsh maybe, but certainly true! The leadership guru, John C. Maxwell, tells us that leadership is all about influence. You may not think you have the gift or passion of leadership, and yet all of us exercise influence in our daily lives, consciously or otherwise. But how serious do we take that responsibility? Are we positively influencing the people around us? Are we positively influencing our world?

Paul reminds us to take our influencing responsibility 'seriously'. The Greek word he uses is *spoude*, which speaks about working hard, striving to give the very best and fully embracing the task. So what does that look like?

Firstly, leaders confront the current situation. they're willing to speak up and challenge the status quo. There's a broken world out there that needs Jesus, so we must not allow indifference, complacency or a desire for comfort to keep us from confronting the darkness.

Secondly, leaders create a compelling future. They paint a picture of a new reality and invite others to join in. American developmental psychologist Howard Gardner says: 'Leadership is the ability to create a story that affects the thoughts, feelings and actions of other individuals.'* People will only ever move from where they are if the joy of the new reality outweighs the pain of leaving the existing reality; if they believe the pain of staying is greater than the pain of changing. Leaders help people move.

Thirdly, leaders cultivate culture ('the way we do things around here'). If the leader acts with love, kindness, generosity, humour, hard work and so on, then that's the culture and atmosphere that will be created. It's the leader's job to create a God-honouring kingdom culture wherever they find themselves. It's amazing how powerful a leader's influence can be if they commit to doing this, because words and actions can be contagious.

Finally, and most importantly, leaders are personally committed to developing a godly character. Good leaders know that God is more interested in their heart than their hands. Jesus often challenged the Pharisees about their lack of integrity. Integrity is all about wholeness of character. The opposite of integrity is a character with holes.

Jesus reminds us in Matthew 23 that true leadership is demonstrated in a life that is growing in grace, humility, commitment, responsibility, honesty, faithfulness and many more such qualities. To lead is to serve and to do this in the power of the Spirit.

* Trevor Waldock and Shenaz Kelly-Rawat, *The 18 Challenges of Leadership* (Harlow, UK: Prentice Hall, 2004)

REA⊏ IT

Read Psalm 23. How does God want to lead you today?

T⊢INK IT

How would you behave differently in your workplace, gym, home or community if you truly believed that God had planted you there to bring kingdom influence?

WR/TE IT

Make a note of one thing that has struck you from today's reading.

_____

_____

_____

_____

⊏RAY IT

Pray for someone who is involved in some form of leadership, that God will increase their kingdom influence and impact in the world.

LIV⊑ IT

Change an environment this week through your consistent words and actions; for instance, smile at people stuck in a queue or affirm a shop assistant.

18

Unselectively kind

ROMANS 12:8

'And if you have a gift for showing kindness to others, do it gladly.'

In his autobiography, Mahatma Gandhi wrote that during his student days he seriously considered becoming a follower of Jesus, after reading the Gospels. He could clearly see how the way of Jesus could be the solution to India's unjust caste system. One Sunday, he decided to visit a local church and chat to the minister about how he could become a Christian. Sadly though, upon arrival, he was refused a seat and told that he might be better off worshipping with his 'own people'. He never went to church again because it seemed that, despite the teachings of Jesus, the Christian community were equally steeped in the caste system. A lack of kindness can have life-changing consequences.

In Psalm 145:17, we're reminded that God

is 'filled with kindness' and when we looked at Romans 12:3, we reflected that one of the best definitions of 'grace' is God's loving kindness. God is not *randomly* kind, He is *completely* kind. He doesn't take a brief moment each day to see if He can do something nice for somebody. Every moment of every day, He pours His loving kindness into a hurting, broken world.

As Paul says earlier in Romans 2:11, 'God is no respecter of persons', meaning He shows no favouritism. God is not *selectively* kind. Jesus was kind to people who in the next moment would turn their back on Him. Remember Jesus knowingly washed the feet of Judas Iscariot just hours before Judas betrayed Him. That's incredible loving kindness and there's nothing random or selective about it.

In our journey of becoming more like Jesus, our goal should ultimately be a *lifestyle* of kindness, not just random or selective acts. In Proverbs 3:3 we're told: 'Never let loyalty and kindness leave you! Tie them around your neck as a reminder. Write them deep within your heart.' It's like the writer is saying: 'Every moment of every day, embrace kindness as a lifestyle. Let it be evident to everybody; like a beautiful necklace around your neck. Not something you put on or take off depending on who you're talking to.' That's challenging – no wonder we're reminded it starts in the heart.

Kindness is one of the fruit of the Spirit mentioned in Galatians 5:22. Wouldn't it be great to start every day praying that God, by His Spirit, would create a bigger, kinder heart in us? Not randomly, selectively or begrudgingly kind but completely kind to all people, in all places, at all times and with a joyful and glad spirit.

REAⅭ IT

Read Jeremiah 31:3. Embrace God's loving kindness today.

TⅢINK IT

Why is kindness such a struggle sometimes?

WR/TE IT

Make a note of one thing that has struck you from today's reading.

⊒RAY IT

Pray that the Holy Spirit will grow kindness as a lifestyle in you.

LIVΞ IT

Take up the challenge of being kind to everyone you meet today without being selective. A day of kindness. Do it again tomorrow. And the next day...

19

Love without walking on by

ROMANS 12:9

'Don't just pretend to love others. Really love them.'

Mother Teresa, the Catholic nun who devoted her life to serve the poor in Calcutta, India, once said this: 'Not all of us can do great things. But we can do small things with great love.' She, of course, did both.

By the time she passed away in 1997, she had helped literally tens of thousands of blind, aged, disabled, homeless and leprous people. She even won the Nobel Peace Prize in 1979 for her humanitarian efforts. But the real prize for her was the people. Loving people, one life at a time, with genuine, authentic, sincere and practical love. That's what Paul is speaking about in today's verse.

It's so easy to fall into the trap of pretending to love. We can pretend to listen to someone when our mind is really elsewhere. We can pretend to pray for someone when in reality we never do. We can pretend to care for someone and yet it never drives us into tangible loving action. We can pretend to be moved by the suffering we see on TV but quickly forget within moments of switching it off.

The Greek word Paul uses for 'love' is *agape*: a selfless, servant-hearted and sacrificial love. This way of loving is how God loves us, evidenced by the cross. This form of love is a verb: a *doing* kind of love. It's active, not passive. It's participating, not spectating.

John, one of Jesus' closest disciples, said this: 'This is how we know what love is: Jesus Christ laid down his life for us. And we ought to lay down our lives for our brothers and sisters. If anyone has material possessions and sees a brother or sister in need but has no pity on them, how can the love of God be in that person? Dear children, let us not love with words or speech but with actions and in truth' (1 John 3:16–18, NIV).

What's John saying here? Talk is cheap; actions speak louder than words. If we really love someone, we will listen to them; we will give them our full attention. If we really love someone, we will pray for them, not just tell them we'll pray. If we really love someone, we will do all that we can to help them with the resources that God has given us. If we really love someone then we'll never just walk by.

But I can't help everybody, I hear you say. Of course you're right. But we can help somebody. That's what Mother Teresa did. And when every day we give ourselves to love others, then – just like Mother Teresa – by the end of our lives we'll discover that we may have loved thousands. Jesus tells us, in John 13:34–35, that this kind of love shows the world that we belong to Him and what He is ultimately like. God is on a mission of love and today He invites us to join Him. What are we waiting for?

READ IT

Read 1 John 4:10. Thank God for His wonderful love today.

THINK IT

Why is it hard to love some people and how can Jesus help you with this?

WR/TE IT

Make a note of one thing that has struck you from today's reading.

_____

_____

_____

_____

PRAY IT

Pray that God will increase your love for others, and that you will show it in practical, loving ways.

LIVE IT

Take a moment to dream up an extravagant, sacrificial, loving action towards someone today – and then do it!

20

Driven to action by injustice

ROMANS 12:9

'Hate what is wrong.'

Someone once said: 'The only thing necessary for the triumph of evil is for good men to do nothing.'

You don't need to look too far today to recognise that there is a lot of evil and suffering in the world. Wars are raging across the planet, fuelled by the lust for power and control. Millions of people die every year from starvation, despite the fact that there is enough food for everyone. Tens of thousands of diseased children die every day, even though cheap medication could have saved their lives. According to the International Labour Organization, over 40 million people are victims of modern slavery. There's a lot of evil in the world today. The big question is: What are *we* going to do about it? What are *you* going to do about it?

In the previous session, we looked at Paul's

instruction for us to love without walking on by. As followers of Jesus, we are to love *what* God loves, and love *how* God loves. But in this second part of Romans 12:9, Paul also reminds us that we need to hate what God hates. If love should drive us to action, then hate should drive us to action too.

Psalm 45:7 reminds us that God loves justice and hates evil. The theme of God's justice runs throughout the whole of the Bible. From Genesis to Revelation, we see time and time again a God who sides with the poor, the oppressed, the excluded, the diseased, the disabled, the orphaned, the widowed and the outcast. God rallies passionately against injustice wherever He finds it, and He expects His people to join Him in His mission to stand against the forces of evil in the world. Shane Claiborne says in his book, *The Irresistible Revolution*: 'The early Christians said if a child starves while a Christian has extra food, then the Christian is guilty of murder.'* That's a strong incentive not to ignore injustice.

If we're going to be people who love justice and hate evil, then the challenge has to start with some self-examination. Are there destructive behaviours in our own lives that God hates, and therefore we need to hate too?

In Proverbs 6:16–20, we read that God hates:

- Pride (when people overestimate themselves and underestimate others)
- Lying (when people don't tell the truth)
- Murderous thoughts and actions
- Selfishness (when self-serving, wicked schemes cause suffering to others)
- Self-indulgence (when people fail to exercise self-control and are quick to embrace sin)
- Quarrels (which break and divide relationships)

We could all probably admit to struggling with these vices from time to time. So it's time to receive God's forgiveness and then, with His help, to live differently because we don't want to personally do anything that He hates. We can pray like King David in Psalm 51:10: 'Create in me a clean heart, O God.' And believe that He will.

'Shane Claiborne, *The Irresistible Revolution* (Grand Rapids. MI, USA: Zondervan, 2006) p164

REA◻ IT

Read Isaiah 1:17. Welcome and accept God's challenge to live a life of justice today.

T⊣INK IT

What are the areas of brokenness in your life, and in the world around you, that God is drawing your attention to?

WR/TE IT

Make a note of one thing that has struck you from today's reading.

_____

_____

_____

▱RAY IT

Pray for someone in authority, that God will stir in them an increased passion for His justice in the world.

LIVⴳ IT

Investigate one injustice issue in the world and then do something about it. Pray. Give. Act. Make your voice count!

21

Let's celebrate the good

ROMANS 12:9

'Hold tightly to what is good.'

William Wilberforce and a group of people known as the 'Clapham Sect' began their vision to 'make goodness fashionable' over two hundred years ago. Among other things, they spent huge amounts of time campaigning for the abolition of slavery. But their focus was not just to speak out against injustice and evil; they also wanted to model a different way of living. Wilberforce once said: 'God Almighty has set before me two great objects, the suppression of the slave trade and the reformation of manners.' Wilberforce believed that modelling Jesus' way of life would captivate and change society.

This is the challenge that Paul presents to us in verse 9. As followers of Jesus, our responsibility is to oppose and stand against what is wrong, as we've already looked at, but it's also to celebrate and shine a light on all that is good in the world. In fact, when Paul tells us to 'Hold tightly' to what is good, the word he uses literally means to 'glue together'. We need to be super-glued to a life of goodness!

But what or who is 'good'? Jesus reminds us in Mark 10:18 that only God is ultimately and completely good. The dictionary defines goodness as being morally excellent, virtuous, upright and honourable – and Jesus was all this and more. Goodness poured out of Jesus in all that He said and did, and He sought to draw out and commend the good in others. When a Roman centurion recognises the authority Jesus carries, in Matthew 8, Jesus commends the officer for his level of faith. When a woman pours perfume on Jesus' feet, in John 12, Jesus affirms her actions.

It might seem that what matters most for many people is getting drunk, being selfish, loving money and ignoring injustice. But Jesus calls us to deliberately live differently, embracing a life of goodness and affirming goodness wherever we see it. Paul reminds us that Jesus has created us to do 'good things' (Eph. 2:10), and Solomon challenges us not to 'withhold good from those who deserve it when it's in your power to help them' (Prov. 3:27).

Too often, Christians can come across as being angry and judgmental, spending much of their time complaining about the morality of the world or other people. Wouldn't it be amazing if followers of Jesus were known by the goodness of their words and actions? If we were known as 'people of celebration', holding tightly to goodness, rather than 'people of condemnation'.

Someone once said: 'It may be that the vast majority of unfulfilled needs that bring sadness, heartache, loneliness and despair into human lives are merely the results of good works left undone.' Don't let that be true of us today!

READ IT

Read Philippians 4:8. Ask the Holy Spirit to prompt you to do good things.

THINK IT

How can you build regular habits that grow 'goodness' in your life?

WR/TE IT

Make a note of one thing that has struck you from today's reading.

_____

_____

_____

_____

▭RAY IT

Pray that God will help you to pursue a life of goodness.

LIV⊏ IT

Actively seek out today an opportunity to do something good that will benefit others – if possible, do it secretly.

22

Loving (and liking) other Christians

ROMANS 12:10
'Love each other with genuine affection'

Picture the scene: the disciples are in the upper
room, having a feast of a meal with Jesus, unaware
that this will be the last meal He enjoys before
His impending crucifixion. It's already been an
emotionally charged evening. Jesus has washed the
feet of every dinner guest and He's just revealed
the betrayer, Judas, who has now fled the building,
ready to turn Jesus in to the authorities.

The atmosphere is tense, with suspicions roused,
and every man is ready to point the guilty finger
at his neighbour – will they become a Judas too?
And then, into this moment, Jesus challenges their
unspoken, judgmental thoughts: 'I am giving you a
new commandment: Love each other. Just as I have
loved you, you should love each other. Your love for
one another will prove to the world that you are my

disciples' (John 13:34–35).

There are two reasons why Jesus' disciples are called to cultivate genuine love and affection.

Firstly, they'll face enough persecution and suffering from *outside* their community. To be at odds with each other as Christians is both stupid and destructive. They need to be *for* each other and not *against* each other.

Secondly, their unity as followers of Jesus is a powerful testimony to the world of what Christ is able to do. One of the incredible things about the Church of Jesus Christ is that it is meant to bring together people of every age, background, story, race, struggle and so on, and unite them in Christ. We shouldn't judge each other, criticise each other, gossip or harbour unforgiveness, because we're all work-in-progress people who have experienced the wonderful, life-giving grace of God. If we don't love like this, Jesus says, then our testimony before the world is trashed.

It's tragic when churches split and Christians fall out. Every time this happens, it's a victory for the evil one, whose primary strategy is to destroy the work of God through division. Jesus reminds us that a divided family will not stand (Matt. 12:25) and we are the family of God! So Paul challenges us, as the family of God, to 'Love each other with genuine affection' (Rom. 12:10) – and he's specifically speaking to followers of Jesus. This whole sentence hinges on two Greek words: *philostorgos* and *philadelphia*. *Philostorgos* represents the fond, loving affection that should be shared within a family. Paul then roots this in *philadelphia*, which speaks of the love of brothers or sisters in Christ.

Every family has its arguments and disagreements but, as Jesus' followers, we're committed to sorting them out – quickly, humbly and lovingly – modelling a different way of being community. It's not enough to say 'I love you but I don't like you'. If we do love them, then we want to try and put things right. Paul challenges us to cultivate genuine, affirming, caring relationships with each other as the people of God.

So the next time someone upsets us in church, remember that we don't just have to forgive them – we have to love them *and* like them!

READ IT

Read John 17:21. Ask God to help you to love *and* like fellow believers.

THINK IT

What would it look like for you to love people you find hard to love?

WR/TE IT

Make a note of one thing that has struck you from today's reading.

PRAY IT

If possible, pray together with a friend that each of you will work hard to keep united with fellow believers.

LIVE IT

Has a fellow Christian upset you recently? Put it right today by forgiving and blessing them.

23

R.E.S.P.E.C.T.

ROMANS 12:10

'take delight in honouring each other.'

It was Aretha Franklin who famously sang:
'R.E.S.P.E.C.T. Find out what it means to me...'

Everybody wants respect, right? People can get
really upset if they sense they're being disrespected.
We only need to watch a few reality TV shows
to know that! But getting respect should always
start with a commitment to *give* respect. But why,
and how, should we honour and respect people –
particularly those who wind us up?

In verse 10, there are three significant Greek
words that Paul uses to drive home his point about
the importance of honouring people.

The first Greek word, *time*, translates as 'placing
a value or price on someone'. The Bible tells us in
Genesis that all people are made in the image of
God. That means that *everybody* has intrinsic worth

and value. Everybody is worthy of respect and honour. When we dishonour people, we dishonour God. It's that simple! Einstein had it right when he said: 'I speak to everyone in the same way, whether he is the garbage man or the president of the university.' Of course, this doesn't mean we will always agree with everything people *do*, but we can still honour them as people created in the image of God and therefore inherently valuable.

Secondly, Paul makes it clear that this giving of 'honour' is not vague and intangible. If we really are committed to honouring people, we will put them first. He uses the Greek word *proēgeomai*, meaning 'preferring someone'. The practical outworking of honouring people is to serve them, prioritise them, and to put their needs above our own – that's a challenge, isn't it? It's the same message that Paul shares in Philippians: 'Don't push your way to the front; don't sweet-talk your way to the top. Put yourself aside, and help others get ahead. Don't be obsessed with getting your own advantage. Forget yourselves long enough to lend a helping hand' (Phil. 2:4, *The Message*).

And finally, Paul uses a third Greek word, *allēlōn*, which is most commonly translated in the New Testament as 'one another'. The point is that *everybody* should be honouring *everybody*. Imagine what the world would be like if everybody was committed to honouring each other, putting the needs of others before their own. The world would be a very different place. No wonder Paul encourages us to 'take delight in honouring each other' – because it truly demonstrates the powerful, upside-down nature of the kingdom of God, which is rooted in self-sacrifice for others and ultimately modelled through Jesus' death on the cross.

So the next time someone irritates us, let's remember that they are made in the image of God and are inherently valuable and worthy of tangible honour. So let's demonstrate honour by putting their needs above our own, showcasing kingdom of God values, and, hopefully, inspiring others to do the same.

READ IT
Read Psalm 8:5.

THINK IT

How can we show honour and respect by what we do and say?

WR/TE IT

Make a note of one thing that has struck you from today's reading.

_____

_____

_____

PRAY IT

Be thankful in prayer that God has crowned you with honour.

LIVE IT

Drop a note to a friend, honouring and affirming them for who they are and what they're doing to live for God.

24

No pain, no gain!

ROMANS 12:11

'Never be lazy, but work hard'

In the creation account of Genesis 1, the Bible reminds us that one of the first things God did after He created Adam and Eve was give them a job. Their job was to tend the garden and steward the earth. The garden was a beautiful place but they had to *work* to keep it that way. Work was good for the garden – because it kept the garden beautiful. And work was good for Adam and Eve – because it gave them purpose. It was Anne Frank who famously said: 'Laziness may appear attractive, but work gives satisfaction.'

Jesus is our role model, and we clearly see that He worked very hard to reveal the kingdom of God. He gave His very best to everything He did: no settling for average and no half-hearted commitments. In the Gospel of John, Jesus tells us that His Father is always at work and that Jesus is always working too (John 5:17). Does this mean we should all be working 24/7? Of course not. Only God can do that. The psalmist says that God never goes to sleep (Psa. 121:3–4). But we're not God, and the Scriptures remind us that we can only give our very best from a place of rest. Adam and Eve were created on the sixth day and their first day was a day of rest – the Sabbath. They were to work hard... but from a place of rest.

There are three reasons why we all need to be totally committed to working hard. Firstly, anything worth having is worth working hard for. If we want a great marriage, we have to work hard. If we want to do well in our job, we have to work hard. If we want to win the tennis tournament at Wimbledon, we have to work hard. If we want to be a faithful follower of Jesus Christ, we have to work hard at it. Paul says in 2 Thessalonians 3:10 that if people are not prepared to work hard, why should they expect to have their needs met? Anything worth having is worth working hard for. No pain, no gain!

Secondly, Paul reminds us in Colossians 3:23 that, ultimately, God is our boss in everything we do – and so it's good to give our very best to our heavenly boss. Particularly because He's the best boss in all the world. He's for us. He's always with us. He's given us all the resources of heaven that we need. He's gracious and compassionate, slow to anger and rich in love. When we don't give our very best to whatever we do, we dishonour our boss – we dishonour God.

The final reason for giving our very best in everything we do is because this is our witness before others. Would we rather people remarked that 'Christians are lazy', or 'Christians are hard-working'? Our actions will influence what people think. To some people, you might be their only example of Christianity. What example will we be?

Jesus' brother, James, tells us in James 4:17 that if we know the good we ought to do, but don't do it – that's sin. Yes, that's right! Laziness is sin; whereas hard, diligent work honours God, is good for us and is a positive witness to others.

REA⊐ IT

Read Psalm 121:3. Be thankful that God never sleeps but is always watching over you.

THINK IT

What's your biggest challenge – to rest more or to work harder? And why?

WR/TE IT

Make a note of one thing that has struck you from today's reading.

_____

_____

_____

PRAY IT

Pray that God will inspire and equip you to give your best to whatever you do.

LIVE IT

Where are you not giving your best at the moment? Think about why that might be and, if possible, determine this week to step it up, with God's help.

25

Have you got *zeo*?

ROMANS 12:11

'serve the Lord enthusiastically.'

Last session, we explored the earlier part of Romans 12:11, with Paul's challenge to work hard and not be lazy. In the second part of verse 11, Paul steps it up a notch and really underlines how important it is that we have this wholehearted, work-hard commitment to our relationship with God.

The word he uses for 'enthusiastically' is the Greek word *zeo*, which means 'passion, to boil with heat, to be hot'. Sometimes this word *zeo* is translated as 'zeal'. When we talk about someone being zealous, words like enthusiastic, fervent, extreme or passionate come to mind. It's as if Paul is saying: 'Make sure your desire to serve God across the whole of your life is at boiling point.'

Israel's most famous and beloved king, David, once wrote a song that includes the line: 'zeal for your house consumes me' (Psa. 69:9, NIV). David loved God so much that his whole being was consumed with God's agenda. No wonder God saw him as a man after His own heart!

So what about us? Is our passion for God *hot* today? Are we firing on all our spiritual cylinders, where every waking moment we're poised for kingdom action, doing what God wants us to do, saying what God wants us to say, going where God wants us to go? Consumed with love for God and His mission in the world? If not, why don't we decide today to raise the temperature in our passion for God. How do we do that?

- By apologising to God for any laziness or complacency, inviting Him to fill us afresh with the Holy Spirit, and offering to be a shining light for Christ in the world.

- By hanging out with some passionate Jesus-followers. That's why it's so important that we gather together. If we're feeling that there's not a lot in our passion tank at the moment, let's spend some time with Christians who will encourage us, build us up and pray for us.

- By getting back into our Bibles, reading the Gospels or diving into Acts. Let's read about what Jesus and the Early Church did, remembering that He wants this work to continue through us. Let God's Word remind us how amazing Jesus is, and what an incredible privilege we have to follow Him.

• By setting ourselves some short-term faith goals that will stretch our faith and grow our passion. These goals could be to grow our prayer time by five minutes a day, or to commit to share our faith with at least one person each week, or to pray with someone, or to work through the Psalms for the next 150 days, or to get involved in a new ministry at church, or something else!

Let's commit to doing something that will help fire us up in faith. As the saying goes: 'If you want something you've never had before, you need to do something you've never done before.'

READ IT

Read 1 Kings 8:23. Ask God to help you be more wholehearted in your faith.

T⊣INK IT

Everyone expresses passion in different ways, according to our personality types. What does a passionate zeo life look like for you?

WR/TE IT

Make a note of one thing that has struck you from today's reading.

_____

_____

_____

⊏RAY IT

Pray that your passion for God will ignite to the next level.

LIV⊨ IT

What would stretch your faith and take you out of your comfort zone? Identify it, do it and see how your passion for God grows.

26

Where's your hope?

ROMANS 12:12

'Rejoice in our confident hope.'

In 1979, film actor and director Woody Allen said: 'More than any other time in history, mankind faces a crossroads. One path leads to despair and utter hopelessness. The other, to total extinction. Let us pray we have the wisdom to choose correctly.' This statement could well apply to many other times in world history when there has been a general feeling of hopelessness about the future.

And yet we all really need hope, don't we? We all need hope because life is not perfect. Of course, there are moments of joy and celebration and happiness, but most of the time, some things in life are going really well and some things are going really badly. Life is never perfect. We live in joy and pain. We experience success and struggle at the same time.

The thing that keeps us persevering – the thing that stops us giving up when it seems like we're stuck in the raging storms of life – is *hope*. Proverbs 13:12 tells us that a lack of hope can make our 'heart sick'. A lack of hope can be completely emotionally crushing.

So in what or in whom should we put our hope today? For Paul, the answer was simple. Jesus is our hope. We can put our hope in God. Why? Because:

- God promises never to leave us (Heb. 13:5).
- God promises to bring us through the trials of life (Isa. 43:1–3).
- God promises that a day is coming when all suffering, sadness, sin and death will be destroyed once and for all (Rev. 21:3–4).

Someone once said: 'God's promises are like the stars; the darker the night, the brighter they shine.'

We can rejoice today – despite whatever struggle we're facing – because in Jesus the 'struggle' days are numbered. We may feel like we're going through hell, but with Jesus by our side, we can be sure we're just passing through. God's hope cannot disappoint us because God cannot break His promises (Rom. 5:5).

The prophet Isaiah reminds us that 'those who

hope in the LORD will renew their strength. They will soar on wings like eagles; they will run and not grow weary, they will walk and not be faint' (Isa. 40:31, NIV). This is a promise for us today. Rejoice in confident hope because God is for us (Rom. 8:31), Jesus is with us (Matt. 28:20), the Spirit of God is in us (John 14:17) and angels are encamped around us (Psa. 91:11). What are we worried about? Let's rejoice in our confident hope in Christ today!

READ IT
Read Psalm 10:17. Thank God that He brings hope to the hurting.

THINK IT
What are you hoping for right now?

WR/TE IT

Make a note of one thing that has struck you from today's reading.

_____

_____

_____

_____

▭RAY IT

Pray that you will experience new levels of God's hope.

LIV⊨ IT

Who do you know who is hurting? Can you do something today to bring hope into their lives? Let's be God's hands and feet of hope!

27

Playing the waiting game

ROMANS 12:12
'Be patient in trouble'

I'm not great at waiting. Patience may be a virtue but it's certainly not my strong point. Minor things like filling up with petrol or standing in long queues generate a mild degree of frustration because they prevent me from getting more important things done.

However, there are other, far more important, things that I get impatient about. I get impatient with suffering and struggle; I want them to end – in my own life and in the lives of others. Jesus reminds us that the sun shines and the rain falls on both the righteous and unrighteous (Matt. 5:45). Good and bad stuff happens whether you're a follower of Jesus or not. The big question is not: Will you face tough times? The big question is: How will you *respond* in tough times?

Paul challenges us here in Romans to be 'patient

in trouble'. And when he's talking about trouble, Paul's not speaking about some tiny pinprick of discomfort; this is full-blown, painful, heart-rending distress. Paul dares to say to us, in the midst of the really painful times of suffering in life: 'Don't give up. Hold on to God. Be brave and endure it, knowing that you will come out the other side.' After all, remember that this verse immediately follows what we looked at last time: 'Rejoice in our confident hope' (Rom. 12:12). In fact, the whole of verse 12 hangs together this way: 'In hope, rejoicing! In tribulation, enduring! In prayer, persevering!'

If we have confident hope, then we will be patient in trouble and that will, in turn, encourage us to keep praying until the trouble comes to an end. The problem today is that we live in a quick-fix culture and we expect God to act accordingly. Perhaps God is not looking to provide easy answers but is looking for people who will wait on Him.

And as we learn to wait, there are three things to remember:

1. Wait patiently (Psa. 37:7). Remember, God is God and we are not.
2. Wait quietly (Lam. 3:25–26). Instead of struggling, striving or fighting against God,

let's recognise that God is able to use even the toughest storms to make us stronger people and more like Jesus. Of course, this isn't about enjoying suffering, but simply recognising how God might be using it to strengthen our faith and character.

3. Wait confidently (Micah 7:7). Our hope is not in ourselves, or even our friends and family. Our hope – our confidence – is in God.

REA◻ IT

Read Psalm 33:20. Embrace the benefits of waiting on God.

T⊟INK IT

Why is waiting so difficult for us? What might expectant waiting look like?

WR/TE IT

Make a note of one thing that has struck you from today's reading.

_____

_____

_____

_____

☐RAY IT

Pray that God will help you to grow in patience.

LIVE IT

Be the answer to someone's prayers! If you can help them, don't let them wait any longer.

28

Why is prayer so difficult?

ROMANS 12:12

'and keep on praying.'

Most of us recognise that prayer is vital to the Christian life, and to growing in faith. Author S.D. Gordon said: 'You can do more than pray, after you have prayed, but you cannot do more than pray until you have prayed.' When asked what the secret was of his spiritual power, Charles Spurgeon replied, 'Knee work! Knee work!' – referring, of course, to prayer. There's simply no escaping the fact: anything significant achieved for God is birthed and sustained in the place of prayer.

Jesus tells the story of a persistent widow who nags an uncaring judge to the point that he eventually succumbs to her demands (Luke 18:1–8). Jesus reminds us that if an unrighteous judge will eventually give in to persistent petition, then how much more will our loving Father God respond to our heartfelt, persevering prayers? Jesus' message is the same as Paul's: keep praying and never give up. The answer might be just around the corner.

It's also the same message that Jesus gives in Matthew 7:7–11. When it comes to prayer, ask and keep on asking, knock and keep on knocking, seek and keep on seeking. Until we get our answer, until the door is opened, until we find what we've been looking for: keep on praying!

Elsewhere, Paul challenges us to pray on all occasions and with all kinds of prayers and requests (Eph. 6:18). Silent prayers, loud prayers, written prayers, sung prayers, tear-stained prayers, joy-filled prayers, Scripture-inspired prayers... Persistent, persevering prayers.

Jacob's dream at Bethel made him aware that God was present with him (Gen. 28:10–17). Prayer is a great opportunity to pause and be conscious that God is present with us. We need to learn to cultivate some prayer habits, so that prayer becomes more natural and we become more aware of the presence of God in the everyday moments of our lives.

We can use the everyday activities of our lives to make connections with God, become aware of His presence and pray. For example, when we wake up, we can give thanks to God for a new day. When we take a shower, we can invite God to cleanse us and fill us afresh with His Spirit. When we brush our teeth, we can ask God to help us use our mouths to build people up and not tear them down. When we get dressed, we can commit ourselves to be ready to be used by God. When we eat, we can thank God for His generous provision in our lives. You get the idea!

Just like Jesus' disciples, we all need to learn how to pray. It takes patience and practice to cultivate a regular, impactful prayer life; so let's not give up. The place of prayer is our primary space to meet with God, to share what's on our heart and to hear what's on His.

READ IT

Read 2 Chronicles 7:14–15. Remember that God listens to your prayers.

THINK IT

What creative ways of praying might help to boost your prayer life?

WR/TE IT

Make a note of one thing that has struck you from today's reading.

_____

_____

_____

_____

PRAY IT

Pray that God will help you to grow in passion for prayer.

LIVE IT

Be courageous and offer to pray for someone you know who isn't a Christian this week.

29

Are you ready to help?

ROMANS 12:13
*'When God's people are in need, be
ready to help them.'*

One of the hallmarks of the Early Church was their
unswerving commitment to each other, which was
demonstrated practically by ensuring no one was in
need. We're told: 'They sold whatever they owned
and pooled their resources so that each person's
need was met' (Acts 2:45, *The Message*).

Acts goes on to say: 'All the believers were one
in heart and mind. No one claimed that any of
their possessions was their own, but they shared
everything they had... And God's grace was so
powerfully at work in them all that *there were no
needy persons among them.* For from time to time
those who owned land or houses sold them, brought
the money from the sales and put it at the apostles'
feet, and it was distributed to anyone who had need'

(Acts 4:32–34, NIV, my emphasis). Wow! What a challenge to our individualistic, consumer world!

But this way of living didn't originate in the New Testament. God's command for His people to look out for each other – and after each other – goes right back to the beginning of the story of Israel. After leaving Egypt, God tells His people that there need never be anyone poor among them because He has blessed them with enough to share (Deut. 15:4).

Over a 1,000 years later, the apostle Paul commends the church in Macedonia for their huge love for the people of God, shown by their ridiculous levels of generosity. Despite the fact that the Macedonian Christians were facing severe trials and poverty themselves, they were overflowing with joy to be able to meet the needs of others (2 Cor. 8:1–5).

How do we get to that place where we are so ready to meet the needs of our brothers and sisters in Christ? First and foremost, it's all to do with being overwhelmingly grateful for the grace of God. We already looked at how 'the *grace of God* was so powerfully at work in them all [the Early Church] that there were no needy persons among them' (Acts 4:33–34, NIV, my emphasis). They were so thankful for God's loving kindness, undeserved favour and excessive generosity towards them, how could they do anything but express that to each other? After all, the goal of our faith is to become more like Christ – and surely that has to begin with how we respond to each other as the people of God?

Paul encourages us to partner together, to wholeheartedly jump into the task of sharing with the people of God, so that the practical needs and necessities for the journey of faith and life are met – for everyone. As God's people and Church, we're encouraged to be the place where no one goes hungry, where everyone has clothing and shelter, where every debt is paid. What a powerful testimony that would be for today's broken world. When we begin to do that, then we'll know that the grace of God has broken out among us.

READ IT

Read Psalm 9:18. Remember that God is on the side of the needy.

THINK IT

What resources has God given you, and how you can you share them to meet the needs of those around you?'

WR/TE IT

Make a note of one thing that has struck you from today's reading.

_____

_____

_____

PRAY IT

Pray together with a friend that you will both step up your commitment to meet the needs of the family of God.

LIVE IT

Meet a practical need for someone in your church this week – but aim to do it secretly.

30

Entertaining angels

ROMANS 12:13

'Always be eager to practice hospitality.'

In the last reading, we saw how Paul directs the
Church to ensure that no one in the family of God
goes without. But here in the second part of verse 13,
he's talking about offering love and hospitality to
strangers. The sentence is actually formed from just
two words in the Greek language: *diōkō philoxenia*.
Diōkō means to wholeheartedly and enthusiastically
pursue, or to run swiftly in order to catch something.
And what's the 'something'? Answer: *philoxenia*
– which means strangers who are in need of love
and hospitality. Paul's message is absolutely clear
and extremely challenging: don't just love friends
and fellow believers; genuine Christlike love *must*
reach out to the stranger, the outcast, the poor and
oppressed, the naked and imprisoned – even the
aggressor or the enemy. In fact, Paul is challenging us

to actively pursue these kinds of people.

Jesus earned Himself the nickname 'friend of sinners' because He regularly dined with the so-called scum of society: prostitutes, tax collectors and lepers. God's love has the wonderful ability to look beyond someone's appearance, history or circumstance, and simply see them as precious and worthwhile. Everyone has dignity in the kingdom of God. In his book *The Ragamuffin Gospel*, Brennan Manning writes: 'It would be impossible to overestimate the impact these meals must have had upon the poor and the sinners. By accepting them as friends and equals Jesus had taken away their shame, humiliation and guilt.'*

In Matthew, Jesus shares a parable about the two types of people who will face God's judgment at the end of this age. There are those – the sheep – who fed the hungry, gave the thirsty a drink, offered kindness to a stranger, clothed the naked, looked after the sick and visited the imprisoned. Jesus commends these people, telling them that when they did these acts of kindness for the 'least' in society, it was as though they were doing it for Christ Himself. Jesus' harshest words are reserved for those – the goats – who refused to show such kindness to a stranger (Matt. 25:31–46). The writer of Hebrews shares the same message by reminding us to show hospitality to strangers because, in doing so, we may be entertaining angels without realising it (Heb. 13:2).

Clearly, the Bible doesn't mean that we are saved by our 'works' of kindness, but genuine faith in Christ needs to be obvious by our actions – particularly in meeting the practical needs of others (James 2:14–17). Imagine the impact the Church would have if every day, every member asked God to help them be hospitable to a stranger? It might look like the kingdom of God had come!

'Brennan Manning, *Ragamuffin Gospel* (Colorado Springs, CO, USA: Multnomah, 2005)

REA⊂ IT

Read Matthew 25:37–40. Remember that serving the needy means serving Jesus.

TⅠINK IT

Are there some prejudices and bad attitudes that you need to face up to, in order that you can become good news to the poor and the stranger?

WR/TE IT

Make a note of one thing that has struck you from today's reading.

PRAY IT

Pray that God will give you boldness to be kind to strangers.

LIVE IT

Commit to an act of hospitality for a stranger every day for the next seven days; for example, buy someone a coffee, sit and chat with a homeless person, or invite a new person at church to lunch or dinner.

31

Love in the face of intolerance

ROMANS 12:14
'Bless those who persecute you.
Don't curse them; pray that God will
bless them.'

The book of Acts tells the inspiring story of the exponential growth of the Early Church, as ordinary men and women did extraordinary things through the power of the Holy Spirit – but it's not all easy reading. The first Christians were regularly threatened, arrested, beaten, tortured, imprisoned and executed. Jesus never promised His disciples a life of comfort and safety. Someone once said, 'Jesus promised His disciples three things: that they would be entirely fearless, absurdly happy, and always in trouble.' Why did the disciples press on in the face of persecution? How could they still be good news to others, even to their persecutors – and even in the face of death? Because they knew that:

- Jesus is the good news that everyone needs to hear (Rom. 1:16).
- Persecution builds maturity in our faith (James 1:2–4).
- Nothing can ever separate us from God – not even death (Rom. 8:35).

What is also inspiring is how the Early Church *responded* to the persecution. There is no record in the book of Acts of the disciples praying that persecution would end. They never complained to God about the hardships they faced. They never retaliated or sought revenge. They never gave up on sharing the good news of Jesus. Instead, they understood that the adventure of following Jesus meant embracing both triumphs and trials. They prayed for boldness in persecution. They rejoiced because they had been counted worthy to suffer for Jesus. They lovingly forgave their persecutors. This is our challenge today: to respond in the very same way.

To a greater or lesser extent, we may also face persecution. Paul writes that 'everyone who wants to live a godly life in Christ Jesus will suffer persecution' (2 Tim. 3:12). In some countries, Christians face imprisonment or worse because of their beliefs. Every day is a challenge to hold fast to the promise that God is always with them. For others of us, persecution might be more subtle: a sarcastic comment about the Bible or our beliefs.

Whatever form of persecution we may encounter, today's verse encourages us to bless our persecutors, to pray that God will reach them with His love and forgiveness in the same way that He reached out to us. Everybody needs Jesus. Our family, our friends, complete strangers... and even our enemies. Let's pray that God will help us, through the power of His Spirit, to respond with love to those who are opposed to the Christian faith. Because when we do, we become a little bit more like Jesus. And who knows what might happen next?

READ IT

Read John 15:18–19. Ask God to give you the strength to endure persecution, just like Jesus.

THINK IT

How comfortable have you become with your faith, and how can you start to take more risks?

WR/TE IT

Make a note of one thing that has struck you from today's reading.

_____

_____

_____

_____

▭RAY IT

Millions of Christians are facing torture and death every year simply because they love Jesus. For more information and prayer suggestions, visit opendoorsuk.org

LIV▭ IT

Is there someone who has been giving you a hard time because of your faith? Can you respond the same way as the disciples did? Pray that God will give you strength to continue to treat them with respect and kindness.

32

If you're happy then I'm happy

ROMANS 12:15
'Be happy with those who are happy'

When we watch the TV or read the newspapers, we might get the impression that our culture today seems to struggle to celebrate the success of others. If young people do really well in their A Levels, then their exams must have been too easy. If a team or individual wins a game, then it must be because the opposition wasn't playing well. Rather than being an encourager, we can easily rob someone of their joy or happiness.

If we're honest, Paul's simple command for us to 'be happy with those who are happy' is not quite as easy as it seems. We live, to varying degrees, with the crippling effects of comparison. It's hard to be happy for someone when we wish that we were the ones who had the 'lucky break'. It's hard to celebrate someone else's success when the success that they've achieved is something we've been longing for ourselves and we feel we continue to miss out on. Sometimes this can be deeply painful; for example, a friend gets a job and yet for months you remain out of work, a couple are having a baby and yet you continue to struggle to conceive, or another friend has got married and yet you're still waiting to find a partner. The list goes on...

In my experience, we can live in two opposite emotions. We *are* pleased for someone but deep down we might also wonder: *Why not me? When will my time come?*

The word for 'happy' that Paul uses here is the Greek word *chairō*, and it's a word that describes wholehearted, passionate rejoicing. No holds barred. No luke-warmness. No tinges of selfishness or cynicism. How can we be *chairō*-type people? How can we break the power of comparison so that we genuinely can rejoice when others are rejoicing?

Firstly, by being thankful because we are blessed. Sometimes we're so concerned about what we *don't* have that we miss out on being thankful for what we *do* have. God loves us. God is for us. God will always be there for us. God will provide for us. We all, like Paul in Philippians 4, need to learn to be more content. We are all blessed in one way or another.

Secondly, be joyful when others are blessed. Jesus tells us that God sends times of sunshine and rain, good times and challenging times, on everybody (Matt. 5:45). If someone is experiencing some good times, then let's celebrate with them – because the next moment we might be weeping with them.

Thirdly, to fully break the power of comparison and self-centredness, pray that others will be even more blessed; that they have even more reasons to rejoice. Pray that they will experience unparalleled levels of God's grace. The more we pray God's blessing on others, and mean it, the more it will kill selfishness and any sense of entitlement in us.

REA⊐ IT

Read 2 Timothy 1:9. Remember that you've been saved by grace; you didn't earn it or deserve it.

THINK IT

In what areas of your life do you struggle with comparison? To whom do you compare yourself?

WR/TE IT

Make a note of one thing that has struck you from today's reading.

_____

_____

_____

_____

PRAY IT

Pray for a friend, that God will bless them beyond their wildest dreams.

LIVE IT

Has someone you know had good news recently? Drop them a card or send them a message to congratulate them.

33

Shed a tear before you speak a word

ROMANS 12:15

'and weep with those who weep.'

Theodore Roosevelt once said: 'No one cares how much you know, until they know how much you care.'

How do we express our care for others? Job's comforters are famous for being the most uncaring, judgmental friends a person could have. Job had lost his business, his kids and his health. Even Job's wife had told him to 'Curse God and die' (Job 2:9). He was going through an agonising time, but his friends, Eliphaz, Bildad and Zophar, still proceeded to blame him for his predicament, assuming that he was being punished by God.

Sometimes the best thing we can do for those who are suffering is to keep our mouth shut, our heart open and just weep with them, which is what makes the story of Job's friends so disappointing after starting off so well. They had agreed to go together to comfort Job, and for the first week that's precisely what they did. They sat with him. Wept with him. They didn't speak a word. They just remained present in Job's suffering (Job 2:11–13). Shame that they then started talking...

Our first response to those who are suffering is not to whip out our best advice, or even our favourite prayer. Nope! Paul encourages us to enter into their pain and weep with them. 'If one part suffers, all the parts suffer with it, and if one part is honoured, all the parts are glad' (1 Cor. 12:26).

Author Henri Nouwen once wrote:

> '...when we honestly ask ourselves which persons in our lives mean the most to us, we often find that it is those who, instead of giving advice, solutions, or cures, have chosen rather to share our pain and touch our wounds with a warm and tender hand. The friend who can be silent with us in a moment of despair or confusion, who can stay with us in an hour of grief and bereavement, who can tolerate not-knowing, not-curing, not-healing and face with us the reality of our powerlessness, that is a friend who cares."

I remember a time when something truly heart-wrenching had happened in our family. A close family friend came round as soon as he heard the news. I'll never forget how he sat with us in stunned, heart-broken silence for maybe an hour, maybe more. Words weren't required. We just needed someone to be present with us in our moment of pain; to weep with us as we wept.

Time and time again we see Jesus moved with compassion for the people He encountered. 'Jesus wept' (John 11:35, NIV) is the shortest verse in the whole of the Bible. Sometimes we think that God is disinterested and disconnected from our suffering, but the God of the Bible is a weeping God. He weeps with us; He weeps for us – and He invites us to do the same for each other.

'Henri Nouwen, *Out of Solitude: Three Meditations on the Christian Life* (Notre Dame, IN, USA: Ave Maria Press, 2004) p38

READ IT

Read Isaiah 40:1. Remember that God longs to comfort His people in their suffering.

THINK IT

What stops you from slowing down, being quiet and simply choosing to be with those who are suffering?

WR/TE IT

Make a note of one thing that has struck you from today's reading.

_____

_____

_____

_____

PRAY IT

Ask God to increase your compassion for those who are suffering.

LIVE IT

Is there anyone you know who is struggling or suffering?

How can you reach out to them without words?

34

Why can't we all just get along?

ROMANS 12:16

'Live in harmony with each other.'

In the film *Mars Attacks*,* Jack Nicholson plays an American president who finds himself at war with an alien army from Mars. As the situation becomes increasingly hopeless, he remarks to the aliens: 'Why can't we work out our differences? Little people, why can't we all just get along?'

Of course, we don't need aliens from outer space to find ourselves asking that question. Spend just a few minutes watching any reality TV programme and you'll see people struggling to 'live in harmony with each other'. The same may be true in our home, school or office, which is why the way of Jesus is so important, challenging and counter-cultural.

The message of our world is often 'love those who love you back', 'help those who help you back' and 'give to those who will give back to you'. But Jesus is deliberately different, and He calls His followers (that's you and me) to follow His example and draw people together rather than push them apart.

So how can we truly live in harmony with other people? The New Testament writers remind us that some of the ways include:

- Encouraging one another – building each other up (1 Thess. 5:11)
- Forgiving one another – because no one is perfect (Col. 3:13)
- Loving one another – in the way Jesus has loved us (John 13:34)

In their book on mentoring, authors Paul Stanley and Robert Clinton quote a respected psychologist who says: 'I am thoroughly convinced that if Christians practised the "one anothers" to any degree at all, 90% of my Christian clients wouldn't need me, and all the others, Christian or non-Christian, would flock to the church where it was happening.'***

Wow! What a challenge!

Most people long to be part of a community where there is harmony, as expressed through the 'one anothers', which requires more than simply willing it to happen. We're all different. We will wind each other up. We will disagree. Unity does not mean uniformity, and we can learn to disagree without becoming disagreeable. Despite our differences and disagreements, we can be committed to supporting, encouraging, inspiring, confessing, forgiving and loving. All of these actions will work towards achieving harmony with others.

Finally, let's remember that God blesses harmony. Psalm 133 tells us that where there is unity, 'GOD *commands* the blessing' (Psa. 133:3, *The Message*, my emphasis). So if we want to experience God's blessing, and pass that blessing on, then let's be people who are committed to living in harmony with others.

*Mars Attacks (Warner Bros., 1996)
**Paul D. Stanley and J. Robert Clinton, *Connecting* (Colorado Springs, CO, USA: NavPress, 2015)

REA⊏ IT

Read Psalm 133. Remember that God blesses unity.

T⊣INK IT

Which of the 'one anothers' do you struggle to put into practice? Ask the Holy Spirit to help you grow in that area.

WR/TE IT

Make a note of one thing that has struck you from today's reading.

_____

_____

_____

_____

⊏RAY IT

Pray that God will help resolve any issues with people that cause disharmony.

LIVᴱ IT

Look for opportunities this week to bring harmony into difficult situations. Choose to make them better, not worse.

35

Making friends with 'nobodies'

ROMANS 12:16
'Don't be too proud to enjoy the company of ordinary people.'

Picture the scene: it's 10.15 on a Sunday morning and the church service is due to start in 15 minutes, when two strangers arrive within moments of each other. The first walks in, sporting a very expensive Armani suit; the waft of his Cartier aftershave and his gold-ringed fingers immediately tell you that this guy is loaded. And he's good looking. He's given a very warm welcome, a guided tour of the church, coffee with cake, and a seat next to the pastor.

The second man walks in, wearing filthy clothes. He's obviously homeless, and from his odour it seems he's not washed in some time. The few remaining teeth he has left are crooked and his breath smells. For a while, he's left standing alone. No one seems as keen to welcome him. When eventually someone does speak to him, he doesn't get the guided tour – after all, perhaps he'll steal something – and he's seated in the corner at the back of the church with an usher flanking him on either side.

Now ask yourself the question: If you were in church that day, how would you have acted? Would you have treated both people exactly the same? Who would you have greeted first? This is the challenge that Paul presents in today's verse and the exact scenario that James paints in James 2:1–10. James has some very strong words for those who are guilty of favouritism, which is probably most of us from time to time, if we're honest.

In James 2:1, James tells us that faith and favouritism are incompatible. Favouritism is unchristian; it's the opposite of being Christlike. In fact, James writes that it's an 'evil' (James 2:4). That makes for uncomfortable reading! Jesus treated everybody with dignity, whether they were rich, poor, healthy, diseased, important or a social outcast – and He commands us to do the same (Luke 14:12–14).

James also reminds us that favouritism is unbalanced because we can end up neglecting the people who need our help the most, the poor and vulnerable, while we pander to the rich. But a person's 'net worth' doesn't determine their 'self-worth'. Everyone is beautiful and precious because everyone is made in the image of God. We need God's help to see people as He sees them.

Ultimately, favouritism is unloving. Jesus shows us that we are to reach out to the last, the least and the lost. The Church must be a place where you are welcome no matter who you are, where you've been or what you've done. The Church must be a place where you can belong regardless of your age, status, wealth, sexuality, religion, disability or ethnicity.

When we see people through the eyes of Jesus, we realise that *everybody is a somebody* and worthy of our time and attention. So who can we reach out to? Who do we usually avoid in favour of closer friends? Dare we take up the challenge to be a friend to the friendless? When we do, the results may be surprising.

REA⬭ IT

Romans 2:11. Be thankful that God does not show favouritism.

151

THINK IT

Who are the 'nobodies' and 'strangers' in your world that you need to reach out to in love?

WR/TE IT

Make a note of one thing that has struck you from today's reading.

_____

_____

_____

_____

PRAY IT

Pray that God will help you see people through the eyes of Jesus.

LIVE IT

Go out of your way this week to be kind to someone you would not normally connect with.

36

No one likes a smarty-pants!

ROMANS 12:16

'And don't think you know it all!'

In Matthew 23, Jesus strongly criticises the religious leaders for not practising what they preach. This is not 'gentle Jesus meek and mild'. He reveals the reality of their compromising, legalistic, hypocritical, irresponsible, complacent and dishonest lives. Jesus repeatedly accuses them of being blind: 'Blind guides' (v16), 'Blind fools' (v17,24), 'blind Pharisee' (v26) and 'How blind!' (v19). This must have been extremely uncomfortable to hear – no wonder the Pharisees wanted Jesus dead. After all, who did Jesus think He was, saying such things to *them*? And yet this was exactly the question Jesus was posing to *them*: 'Who do you think you are? You're steeped in pride. You think you know it all but the reality is you know nothing! Stop trying to be a great somebody!'

The Apostle Paul must have had a similar concern for the Christians in Corinth because he repeatedly returns to this challenge throughout his first letter to them: 'Don't fool yourself. Don't think that you can be wise merely by being up-to-date with the times. Be God's fool – that's the path to true wisdom. What the world calls smart, God calls stupid' (1 Cor. 3:18–19, *The Message*).

Knowledge doesn't impress God, particularly when it's only used to make someone look good. It's so true of our world today, isn't it? People even talk about how 'knowledge is power'. If I know something that you don't know, then I have the upper hand – I'm better than you. Paul makes it clear that knowledge isn't power; the greatest power in the universe is love. He writes: 'while knowledge makes us feel important, it is love that strengthens the church. Anyone who claims to know all the answers doesn't really know very much. But the person who loves God is the one whom God recognizes' (1 Cor. 8:1–3). Paul goes on to say that over-confidence in ourselves puts us at great risk of messing up: 'So, if you think you are standing firm, be careful that you don't fall!' (1 Cor. 10:12, NIV).

Sadly, there are far too many examples of high-profile Christian men and women who have given the impression of being infallible but then have spectacularly messed up, damaging themselves and their closest relationships in the process. And before any of us sit in judgment on these folks, remember that if we don't think this could ever happen to us, then we're guilty of falling into the same trap.

There are no know-it-all's in the kingdom of God – except God Himself. The rest of us are learners. We're depending on God to lead us, guide us and teach us how to become more like Jesus. We need to be living a life of love that makes Jesus look good, rather than trying to turn the attention onto ourselves. After all, 'God opposes the proud' (James 4:6), meaning that God is against us if our heart is full of pride. Surely that's important enough for us to daily make sure that we're trying to kill pride in our life and live a life of love?

READ IT

Read 1 Chronicles 29:17 and let God examine your heart.

THINK IT

What areas of pride do you need freeing from in your life?

WRITE IT

Make a note of one thing that has struck you from today's reading.

_____

_____

_____

_____

PRAY IT

Pray that the Holy Spirit will make you aware of any pride in your life and help you become more humble.

LIVE IT

Who are the 'outsiders' in your community that tend to be looked down on? Why not get to know them and find ways to regularly connect with them.

37

No more tit-for-tat

ROMANS 12:17

'Never pay back evil with more evil.'

Have you ever been driving along at the speed limit when another car pulls up *really* close to the back of your car, obviously impatient and frustrated that you're not going faster? How do you respond? Do you just keep at the speed limit? Or do you decide to slow down and wind them up even more?

Have you ever been in an argument with a friend and then they have stopped talking to you? How do you respond? Do you reach out and try to reconcile? Or do you give them the silent treatment back? If they can't be bothered to talk to you, then you can't be bothered with them.

Have you ever sent someone a birthday or Christmas card, only to be disappointed that you didn't receive one back yourself? How do you respond? Keep sending them cards anyway? Or do you wipe the person off your card list?

How we respond to people who have not treated us well is the theme of today's verse. According to Matthew, the golden rule is to 'Do to others whatever you would like them to do to you' (Matt. 7:12). This often goes against our natural inclination to treat them the same way as they treated us.

During Jesus' time on earth, the religious community held to the Old Testament principle of 'an eye for an eye'. But to be clear, the principle of 'an eye for an eye' was *not* God commanding retribution. In fact, it was the very opposite. The principle of 'an eye for an eye' was all about exercising restraint to avoid an out-of-control descent into violence and death. (For instance, 'You killed my brother, so I'll kill all of your family.') Into this world, Jesus then takes this principle of restraint to another level. In the Sermon on the Mount, Jesus says: 'Here's another old saying that deserves a second look: "Eye for eye, tooth for tooth." Is that going to get us anywhere? Here's what I propose: "Don't hit back at all." If someone strikes you, stand there and take it. If someone drags you into court and sues for the shirt off your back, giftwrap your best coat and make a present of it. And if someone takes unfair advantage of you, use the occasion to practice the servant life. No more tit-for-tat stuff. Live generously' (Matt. 5:38–42, *The Message*).

This presents a huge challenge to our human nature. Won't we just be like a doormat if we allow people to treat us this way? What on earth was Jesus thinking? Answer: reconciliation. God is in the business of reconciliation and restoring relationships. He commands us to embrace actions that are restorative, not retributive.

Jesus is our great example in this. As He hung in agony on the cross, abused and mocked by the angry crowd, it would have been so easy – and even understandable – if He had called down fire from heaven to destroy those who treated Him with such contempt. But no! Jesus' response was revolutionary: 'Father, forgive them, for they don't know what they're doing' (Luke 23:34). He commands us to make the same response. So let's not pay back evil with evil but let's commit to reconciliation.

READ IT

Read 2 Corinthians 5:19 and be thankful that God is committed to reconciliation.

T⊢INK IT

What are the barriers to reconciliation between individuals, and how can they be overcome?

WR/TE IT

Make a note of one thing that has struck you from today's reading.

_____

_____

_____

_____

⊏RAY IT

Pray that God will help you to embrace reconciliation in difficult relationships.

LIV⊑ IT

Is reconciliation needed in any of your family or friend relationships? Courageously be the one who makes the first move this week.

38

Shine bright like a diamond

ROMANS 12:17
'Do things in such a way that everyone can see you are honorable.'

Some people are so desperate for fame that they would do anything to get attention on TV or views on YouTube. In fact, such people are called 'infamous', meaning they have an extremely bad reputation due to their poor behaviour. Sadly, poor behaviour is not just limited to TV programmes; people with bad reputations can be found in every place, including our homes and even churches. It's probably why the author Brennan Manning said: 'The greatest single cause of atheism in the world today is Christians: who acknowledge Jesus with their lips, walk out the door, and deny Him by their lifestyle. That is what an unbelieving world simply finds unbelievable.'

This is the challenge that Paul is speaking about

in today's verse. We are called to live a head-turning life, not because we're living dishonourably but because we're living so deliberately differently from the world. We're living like Jesus. The Greek word that Paul uses to describe the kind of life we're supposed to live is *kalos*. This is a word loaded with multiple meanings: good, beautiful, excellent, eminent, precious, useful, suitable, commendable, admirable, magnificent, genuine, praiseworthy, noble, agreeable and honourable. Of course, living such a life is impossible without God's help but that's why He has given us the Holy Spirit to help us to live like Jesus in the world.

Jesus said: 'let your good deeds shine out for all to see, so that everyone will praise your heavenly Father' (Matt. 5:16). What a challenge! Paul and Jesus both spoke about the importance of living a 'stand out' life. It's good for us. It's good for those around us. But the main point is that it directs people to God. It's about making Him famous – not us. That's why it's so counter-cultural.

If people ask us, 'Why do you live deliberately different?' our answer shouldn't be, 'Because we are awesome!'. Our answer needs to be, 'Because God is awesome and He is healing my brokenness and helping me live right!'

Peter gives similar advice: 'Be careful to live properly among your unbelieving neighbors. Then even if they accuse you of doing wrong, they will see your honorable behaviour, and they will give honor to God when he judges the world' (1 Pet. 2:12). So let's be committed to living a head-turning life, but for the right reason: that as people look at us, they will be inspired to look to God.

READ IT

Read Galatians 5:22–23. Ask God to help you embrace the fruit of the Spirit in your life.

THINK IT

What things can you say and do to make Jesus more famous in your world?

WR/TE IT

Make a note of one thing that has struck you from today's reading.

_____

_____

_____

_____

PRAY IT

Pray that God will help you to live honourably for Him in the world.

LIVE IT

How could the light of your life shine brighter this week? For example, maybe you could change the atmosphere in a room by smiling and welcoming people. Think of one thing. Pray. Do it. Give God the credit.

39

Be a peacemaker

ROMANS 12:18

'Do all that you can to live in peace with everyone.'

Someone once said: 'The more I get to know the human race, the more I love my dog.' Sometimes it's easy to understand where this person is coming from. Dogs are considered faithful, dependable, eager to make us happy and quick to forgive our faults; no wonder we call them 'man's best friend'. Don't you wish more people were like that?

But people aren't like that a lot of the time. People wind us up and let us down. They're silent when we need them to speak up, and they often say too much when we need them to be quiet. They're argumentative, always wanting to be right and hating to be wrong. They can get hot-headed and cold-hearted, wounding us with words that cut us like daggers. Who are these people? Take a look in the mirror, because we *all* can be like this at times. I'm describing people just like you and me.

In today's verse, Paul challenges us to live differently: to be peacemakers and not troublemakers. Our words and actions should be making things better, not bitter. We're called to be those who restore relationships, not wreck relationships. We're joining Jesus in His ministry of reconciliation, which is why Jesus says, 'God blesses those who work for peace, for they will be called the children of God' (Matt. 5:9).

When we work to bring peace, we're behaving like our heavenly Father's children. People will see the family resemblance because this is what God is like; this is what God does. God is in the business of developing healthy community.

James, Jesus' brother, reminds us: 'You can develop a healthy, robust community that lives right with God and enjoys its results *only* if you do the hard work of getting along with each other, treating each other with dignity and honor' (James 3:18, *The Message*).

In these verses, James gives us some keys to being a peacemaker:

- Recognise that being a peacemaker is hard work. Let our words and actions be directed towards treating people well, even if we don't feel like it.
- Recognise that everyone is made in the image of God and is precious to God, so treat each other with dignity and honour.
- Remember that forgiveness is always the first step towards reconciliation.

Paul makes it clear in today's verse that our response is our responsibility: 'Do all that you can'. Other translations phrase it: 'as much as *is possible* on your part' (Jubilee Bible 2000). Paul recognises that sometimes we might have done everything we can, and yet we don't achieve peace with someone. That's because it always takes two people to reconcile, while it only ever takes one person to forgive. Our responsibility is to forgive and act in a way that demonstrates our forgiveness – the rest lies with them!

READ IT

Read Romans 5:1 and remember you have peace with God.

THINK IT

In what situations, and with what people, do you struggle choosing peacemaking over troublemaking?

WR/TE IT

Make a note of one thing that has struck you from today's reading.

_____

_____

_____

_____

PRAY IT

Pray that God will help you to be a peacemaker.

LIVE IT

Are you aware of any relationship conflicts? Is there something you can do that will help reconciliation?

40

Leave it with God

ROMANS 12:19

'Dear friends, never take revenge. Leave that to the righteous anger of God. For the Scriptures say, "I will take revenge; I will pay them back," says the LORD.'

'Revenge is a dish best served cold.' Where did that saying come from? If you search the internet, you'll find all manner of different suggestions. In the film *Star Trek II: The Wrath of Khan**, I like that it's referred to as an old Klingon saying, but I'm sure there are other more accurate sources!

What does the saying mean? It's suggesting that the best kind of revenge is delivered in a cold-hearted, grudge-bearing kind of way. Do your worst to your enemy. Get even and get happy. But is that actually the way revenge works?

There's an old Chinese proverb, credited to Confucius, which says: 'Before you embark on a journey of revenge, dig two graves.' If you're embracing cold-hearted revenge, then all you're going to end up with is a cold heart, and as far as I'm aware (with my limited biological knowledge), a cold heart is a dead heart. And who wants a dead heart?

The Bible repeatedly commands us to resist revenge at all costs. God knows that if we start playing revenge games, we'll quickly discover that the game never ends and the only 'prize' is a trail of increasing hurt, bitterness and broken relationships.

So how can we let go of our desire or intent for revenge? Answer: dare to leave it with God. Today's verse is God basically saying: 'Let me pick it up! Let me handle it!' Solomon wrote similar words in Proverbs: 'Don't say, "I will get even for this wrong." Wait for the LORD to handle the matter.' (Prov. 20:22)

So why should we leave it with God? Three reasons from three different people:

1. Job reminds us that 'true wisdom and power are found in God' (Job 12:13). Only God is truly wise and so He *alone* knows the best way to handle a situation – or a person.

2. Moses reminds us everything God does is 'just and fair' (Deut. 32:4) – far more fair than we could ever be. God doesn't turn a blind eye to

injustice but neither is He quick-tempered or vindictive.

3. The psalmist reminds that God 'is righteous in everything he does' (Psa. 145:17). We can trust that God will do the right thing.

So the next time we're tempted to get our own back on someone, let's pause, pray and leave it with God. Let's trust in His wisdom, justice and righteousness to handle the matter, understanding that God is always wanting to heal and restore the brokenness in our world and in all people. Let's be grateful that the grace and mercy with which God responds to others is the same grace and mercy He directs towards us.

¹*Star Trek II: The Wrath of Khan* (Paramount Pictures, 1982)

REA⊂ IT

Read Psalm 36:6. Reflect on the justice and righteousness of God.

T⊢INK IT

If you have chosen revenge over forgiveness in the past, how has that choice affected you personally?

WR/TE IT

Make a note of one thing that has struck you from today's reading.

_____

_____

_____

_____

PRAY IT

Pray that God will free you from the need for revenge. Tell Him about your sorrow and pain, and leave it at His feet.

LIVE IT

Are you nursing acts of revenge or wishing the worst on anyone? Be honest. Pray God's blessing on them and be kind to them.

41

Treat your enemies well

ROMANS 12:20

'Instead, "If your enemies are hungry, feed them. If they are thirsty, give them something to drink. In doing this, you will heap burning coals of shame on their heads."'

In the last reading, we looked at resisting the urge to take revenge and instead choosing to forgive. But Jesus also reminds us that we should be proactively praying for our enemies on a regular basis: 'You have heard that it was said, "Love your neighbour and hate your enemy." But I tell you, love your enemies and pray for those who persecute you, that you may be children of your Father in heaven' (Matt. 5:43–45, NIV). Offering genuine, heartfelt prayers for our enemies is one of the things that demonstrate that we are followers of Christ. But even that is not enough. Jesus says: 'Love your enemies! Do good to them. Lend to them without expecting to be repaid' (Luke 6:35).

Today's verse gives specific examples of how we are to love our enemies, which is so radically different from the way of the world. Meet the needs of our enemies. Blow them away with generous love. But why would anyone do this? Perhaps the notion of feeding our hungry enemy or giving them a drink is not that appealing, but how about heaping burning coals on their head? Let's just press the pause button a second. The burning coals idea is a metaphor, not a command to set fire to the hair of your enemy! In the Bible, when people recognised they had done something terribly wrong and had to change, they sometimes covered themselves with ash. It was a sign of repentance. Paul is saying that the radical love we demonstrate to our enemies, which is totally undeserved, will hopefully bring them to a place of radical repentance; they will realise the error of their ways and change.

Of course, there is wisdom needed. We don't want to put ourselves in a vulnerable position where our enemy can do yet more damage. This is not about accepting abusive relationships. It's simply the challenge of considering how we can be loving and kind to those who behave in the very opposite manner. This is exactly what Jesus did. He washed the feet of Judas just hours before Judas was going to betray Him. And He cried out to God the Father from the cross, inviting forgiveness for the very people who, in that moment, were laughing at His agony. This is the way of Jesus. Love our enemies. Pray for them. Do good to them.

REAᑐ IT

Read 1 Peter 3:9. Ask God to help you thoughtfully respond, and not spontaneously react, to unkindness from others.

THINK IT

What needs to change in you in order for you to love your enemies more easily?

WR/TE IT

Make a note of one thing that has struck you from today's reading.

_____

_____

_____

_____

▭RAY IT

Pray that God will show you how to love your enemies in practical ways.

LIV═ IT

Has anyone really hurt you through their words or actions? Is there a relationship where you keep your distance? What could you do in the next week to surprise that person with a loving act?

42

You can make a difference!

ROMANS 12:21

'Don't let evil conquer you, but conquer evil by doing good.'

And so we come to the end of Romans 12, an incredible chapter that provokes us to think about how we love God, love ourselves and love others, and challenges us to become all that we have been made to be – with the power of God's Spirit. To love God completely, to love ourselves correctly and to love others compassionately is what we were made for, what we were born for and is the reason that we're here today. This is what it means to live a *zeo* life – a life that is burning with passion for God in the world.

We don't need to look too far to know that this world is in trouble and evil abounds. We're reminded every day how broken and far from God many people are, and it's easy to become pessimistic, hopeless and apathetic. It's easy to be deceived into thinking that evil has won. But with Christ, we *can* conquer evil, we *can* overcome and we *can* make a difference.

Whenever we do something with God and for God, it counts and it matters – however big or small.

Paul gives us this powerful encouragement: 'my dear, dear friends, stand your ground. And don't hold back. Throw yourselves into the work of the Master, confident that nothing you do for him is a waste of time or effort' (1 Cor. 15:58, *The Message*).

Isn't that great? Nothing we do for Him is a waste of time or effort. So let's not believe that evil has got the victory or fall for the lie that suffering and struggle have the last word. Let's remember how God's story will end. Revelation chapters 20–21 promise us that evil will be defeated once and for all. In the meantime, every outworking of God's goodness, through me and you, brings that day a little closer.

When we looked at verse 9, we read the quotation: 'The only thing necessary for the triumph of evil is for good men to do nothing.' Don't let that be true of us. Let's do something with God and let's see what God will do. As we close, I invite you to soak in these words from Hebrews, and may God indeed shoot the adrenalin of the Spirit into all our souls.

> *'Do you see what this means—all these pioneers who blazed the way, all these veterans cheering us on? It means we'd better get on with it. Strip down, start running—and never quit! No extra spiritual fat, no parasitic sins. Keep your eyes on* Jesus, *who both began and finished this race we're in. Study how he did it. Because he never lost sight of where he was headed— that exhilarating finish in and with God—he could put up with anything along the way: Cross, shame, whatever. And now he's* there, *in the place of honor, right alongside God. When you find yourselves flagging in your faith, go over that story again, item by item, that long litany of hostility he ploughed through.* That *will shoot adrenaline into your souls!'* (Heb. 12:1–2, *The Message*).

Live Life 1-2-3

Someone once said: 'Never doubt that a small group of thoughtful, committed citizens can change the world. Indeed, it is the only thing that ever has.'

Today, there are over two billion Christians in the world. But it all started with Jesus doing life with a handful of people. It's amazing what can happen over the decades and centuries when you start small. How do you change the world? One life at a time!

One person you're learning from who can help you grow in faith and challenge you to become everything that God created you to be.

Two people to share life with regularly; people who will advise you, pray for you and keep you on track.

Three people that you are leading to live like Jesus in the world, inspiring each of them to share their faith with others.

Small, intentional, accountable, disciple-making relationships are essential to seeing the kingdom of God grow. Could you imagine what might happen if thousands of followers of Jesus across the UK, and beyond, embrace Live Life 1-2-3?

For resources to equip and inspire you, visit **livelife123.org**